TOO MUCH AID, NOT ENOUGH HELP

For Agnes and Tommy, my Mum and Dad, who through their examples taught me so much about justice.

Ken Gibson

Too much Aid:
Not enough help

the columba press

First edition, 2010, published by
the columba press
55A Spruce Avenue, Stillorgan Industrial Park,
Blackrock, Co Dublin

Cover by Ross Print Services
Origination by The Columba Press
Printed in Ireland by
Colour Books Ltd, Dublin

ISBN 978 1 85607 712 5

The views expressed in this work are those of the author and do not necessarily represent the views of The Leprosy Mission Ireland or any other organisation with which he is associated.

Acknowledgements

This book could not have reached completion without the support and help of others.

My wife, Jane, and our children, Nomi, Mary-Beth, Bradley, Jazper and Hunter have been patient and consistent in their sacrifices. Without their dedication, commitment and partnership I could not function in any meaningful capacity.

I owe a huge debt to the Board of The Leprosy Mission Ireland. It is my privilege to work with such a group of amazing, dedicated and compassionate people who strive to serve the world's most marginalised. They have afforded me a real opportunity to learn about, understand and engage with these issues.

My colleague and true friend, Marina Lalor, deserves special acknowledgement for her commitment beyond the call of duty. Her painstaking proofing was invaluable. Any proofing errors that remain are solely my responsibility.

My friends and colleagues at USPG Ireland, Linda and Jan, have 'been there' throughout the life of this project. Their gentle comments, feedback and encouragement have been of more value than they care to imagine.

Of course, sincere thanks are owed to the countless men, women and children I have met across the world. They have shared their experiences, their personal stories, their trials, their hardships … and their enduring hope. They have been an inspiration and a driving force. I hope and pray that, at least in some small way, this book serves their cause.

Contents

Foreword

The motivation for this book grew out of a sense of frustration with the false and inaccurate perceptions many people have about aid. One of my primary aims is to help to debunk the myth that all aid is intrinsically good. Some might feel, as head of a development agency, I am the last person that should undertake such an enterprise. However, it is precisely because of my position that I had to undertake this project to help to protect and defend the integrity the work I do with my colleagues across the developing world. This is because books are starting to appear, one of which even made the bestsellers list recently, which appears to suggest or imply that all aid is bad. Such a simplistic approach is dangerous and, quite frankly, inexcusable at a time of economic crisis because it could cost lives.

Aid can and has delivered some very significant results. No one can dispute the value and impact of The Expanded Programme of Immunization. Launched in 1974, this programme can boast success in increasing the rate of vaccination against six key diseases from 5% of children, to 75% of children by 1990.[1] In practical, day to day terms the impact of this programme continues, saving an estimated 3 million lives a year, and preventing a further 750,000 children a year from becoming permanently disabled. This, and a host of other targeted initiatives have delivered achievements that are to be celebrated. These achievements do not, however, mean that all aid, in all circumstances, is good. Neither do they imply that all aid is necessarily benevolent or well intentioned. Aid is a complicated business. There are many players, each with their own agenda.

But let me be very clear and unequivocal about my position: those of us who work in development and are responsible for

---

1. Glennie 2008: 28

facilitating the transmission of aid to the poor in the developing world have a huge responsibility to call it like it is. Indeed, to put this issue in context, it is worth remembering that many people, not directly involved in development work, believe that most of the aid that goes to help the poor in the developing world is actually transmitted through development agencies, when only 4% of the total is managed in that way. Therefore when people read criticism, often valid, of aid and aid policies it is very important that they realise that 96% of all aid is delivered on a government to government or multilateral basis, and most of the criticism is usually focused in that direction.

The central problem for many working in development agencies is that they also receive their budget allocations from their own governments out of the same national 'aid budget' that is used for bi-lateral and multi-lateral aid transfers. These latter transfers are often made, officially, to help poor countries out of poverty. In reality they are so laden with conditionalities that they advance the interests of the donor and not the recipient country. This book is an attempt to show how that situation has evolved, and how it betrays the noble aspirations and good intentions of the voters who support the stated aims of the aid that is given in their names.

In recent years aid flows have increased. That they have often advanced the interests of the donor institutions and governments only makes it more urgent that those involved in development work speak out. We can see firsthand how the forcing of what are called 'Neoliberal' policies on developing countries has served to make weak states even weaker. These economic policies emphasise tariff free markets, privatisation of public services and the undermining or reduction of the role of the state in the economy. This is a form of full blooded 'Neoliberalism' enforced upon developing nations by developed nations. At the same time, developed countries choose not to force the same policies upon their own economies.

I recognise that developing countries want to develop their economies. I believe they have a right to do so, in their own way. They should not have to accept the model that major international financial institutions like the World Bank and the IMF impose on them, not least because it has not worked and in some cases clearly has made their situation worse. In practical terms, this means that the poor have become poorer, especially in parts of Africa.

In this book I have sought to offer something different in terms of suggesting a way forward. Ultimately the people of the developing world will determine their own destinies. My approach is to focus on ways in which we can begin to make that easier for them. This is in contrast to the present global order which, with some notable exceptions, is much more geared to imposing a model that clearly is designed to favour donor rather than recipient countries.

Ken Gibson

CHAPTER ONE

Introduction

In the first decade of the twenty-first century a new determin-
ation to address poverty and inequality in developing countries
swept the globe. With the economies of developed nations
stronger than they had been at any time in history, and with the
wealth of individuals within those countries also reaching new
highs, there was a genuine sense that the world really could
change for the better, and for everyone. Following decades of
false dawns the climate now appeared perfect to address global
poverty and underdevelopment in a significant and lasting way.
The resentment that had often pervaded the general population
of a country when its government gave large amounts of money
to poorer nations had been greatly diminished by the healthy
economic climate. Many world leaders were also drawn to the
idea of leaving behind a lasting personal legacy. It was a perfect
storm. Everyone, at every level seemed to be involved: church
groups at a local level, charitable organisations at a national level,
and governments at a world level. There was a tangible sense that
the world was on the verge of a fair and permanent transformation.

World leaders such as Tony Blair rallied to this new cause by
stating that a fair settlement for developing nations was inextric-
ably linked to sustained prosperity and security for the rest of the
world. Tony Blair established the *Commission for Africa* (CFA),
which in 2005 reported that, 'It is in our common interests to make
the world a more prosperous and secure place.'[1] The gathering
momentum for change was given focus through *The Millennium
Summit of the United Nations General Assembly*, which convened in
2000. The process that began in 2000 reached a high point in 2005
at the G8 summit at Gleneagles in Scotland. The *Make Poverty*

---

1. CFA, 2006:1, in, Bush, 2007:43

History campaign, that was established in 2005 to coincide with the summit, helped to generate public awareness of just how important the issues being discussed there were. *Make Poverty History* was a resounding success, due in no small part to the great number of celebrities, charities, religious organisations, trade unions, and other interested groups, that actively played a part in the campaign. The associated advertising campaign that ran on television and in the international press helped to ensure that the Summit in Gleneagles was one of the most widely followed in the history of the G8.

The G8 summit at Gleneagles was important in that the issues discussed were scrutinised by many ordinary people. It was, however, the United Nations *Millennium Summit* in 2000 and its agreement upon the *Millennium Development Goals* (MDGs) that gave Gleneagles the bedrock on which it could build. It is unlikely that Gleneagles could have been as successful in the absence of the spirit that the Millennium Summit fostered. The most important MDG agreed in 2000 was the pledge by many world leaders to eradicate extreme poverty and hunger across the world. Other goals included: achieving universal primary education; promoting gender equality and empowering woman; reducing child mortality; improving maternal health; combating diseases such as HIV/ AIDS and Malaria; ensuring environmental sustainability; and developing a global partnership for development.[2]

The MDGs provided donors, non-governmental development organisations (NGDOs), international organisations connected to various governments, and underdeveloped country states with something tangible on which to focus their efforts. Realising these goals became the linchpin in the ensuing global development agenda with widespread agreement on just how momentous the attainment of the goals would be in the advancement of humanity. Never before, outside of war, had so many individuals and groups worked so closely with common purpose, and for the common good.

The outcomes of these processes, as exemplified through the MDGs, provided a focal point towards which governments and

2. See *The Leprosy Mission*, 2009 for a discussion of how much progress has been made so far towards meeting these goals.

organisations could work. However, the MDGs themselves did not provide a clear strategy for how the goals would or could be achieved. On the surface, Gleneagles was a runaway success. It looked as if the issue of poverty was finally going to be consigned to history. All that stood in the way of success, it appeared, was money. In order to attain the lofty goals set out in the MGDs it was estimated that the more developed countries would have to increase aid to 0.7% of their Gross National Income. This increase was supported at Gleneagles by development organisations and advocacy groups, and developed countries were put under pressure to meet this increased level of aid giving.

'The G8 summit was previewed as the moment when the major industrialised capitalist states would usher in a Marshall plan for Africa,'[3] The G8 leaders agreed to double aid to $50 billion a year. This figure made for pleasing headlines, but the *Make Poverty History* campaign that had lobbied for the 0.7% increase pointed out that only $16 billion of the money that had been pledged was actually new funding. It was widely accepted by those interested in fulfilling the MGDs that the new funding package would only partially meet the goals of MGDs. Some groups suggested that the funding package was so inadequate that meeting the MGDs would be impossible. The Millennium Development Project stated that $90 billion a year would be required to attain the MDGs, while other groups put the figure required somewhere in the region of $200 billion a year. Even if they did not agree with the level of aid approved by the G8 leaders, the interested groups did enthusiastically agree with the rhetoric of the donors. That rhetoric vehemently insisted that aid would promote development in poor countries, lifting them out of poverty once and for all. The rhetoric was also adamant that development in poor nations would only be achieved through the benevolence of the rich, industrialised countries. Economic growth in poor countries was seen as the key mechanism that would lead to the achievement of the MDGs.[4] Specifically, it was believed that unprecedented levels of Official Development Assistance (ODA), from rich to poor countries,

3. Bush, 2007: 37
4. Chapter 7 of this book provides a critical discussion of this strategy

would be required to promote sufficient economic growth for poor countries to achieve the goals.

On the surface it was a very simple plan to which all could agree, even if there wasn't universal agreement on the amount of money needed to see the plan through to completion. Poor countries would be lifted out of poverty when rich nations handed over vast sums of money, in an entirely unselfish act. The plan was roundly applauded by most groups, and the world collectively sighed with relief. Humanity had finally grown-up and a new world order based on hope and opportunity for all would be the result. A large portion on the development aid would go towards improving infrastructure, modernising industry, and other projects aimed at increasing the overall wealth of a country. The underlying theory was that once the business backbone of a country was strong enough, then wealth would eventually trickle down to everyone living in that country.

Did the reality live up to the ambition? Did the billions in aid lead to a better standard of living for some of the most vulnerable nations on earth? The answer is no. If rich nations do not take a hard look at the way they approach the giving of aid to poor nations, then the answer to this question will always be no. The problem is a lot more complicated than money, no matter how large the sums involved, can fully address. Gleneagles and other international and national commitments have built a powerful engine for eliminating poverty, but wastage, inefficiency, bureaucracy and corruption has greatly reduced the power of that engine.

This book is concerned with critiquing Official Development Aid (ODA).[5] It will argue that, as a result of both intended and unintended consequences, the bulk of aid often delivers results that benefit the rich rather than the poor. Its primary concern is with bilateral (government to government) and multilateral aid (donations from several governments going to a number of poor

---

5. This is not a book about how charities and Non Governmental Agencies (NGOs) and charities utilise funds given to them by either the public or their respective governments. NGOs can be a mixed bag, some incredibly good stewards, others less so. But that's a topic for another publication.

nations), which makes up the bulk of Development Assistance Committee (DAC) countries' aid disbursements. In commenting on this aspect of aid it is very easy for the message to be oversimplified. There is a danger, in our society driven by sound bites and shocking headlines, that the message can be misheard. This book is critical of some aspects of aid, but that does not mean that all aid in all circumstances is wrong. That would be a gross misrepresentation that could have far-reaching and devastating long term consequences for poor nations and their vulnerable citizens. It is important, however, that we critically examine the 'business' of aid to assess its use, see if it achieves the purpose for which it is intended and figure out how it can be used most effectively.

Charitable donations in the form of aid provided by governments, or through the individual dipping into their wallets and handing over some of their hard earned cash, are commonly viewed as the right things to do. So much so in fact that charitable giving has become somewhat of a sacred cow, and any kind of criticism, no matter how well-meaning or justified, is a taboo. It is only right that nations and individuals should contribute towards eliminating poverty in developing countries, but it's reasonable that those who fund these endeavours, taxpayers and individual contributors, should be provided with clear information on what their efforts are achieving. If a rogue charity is exposed it becomes a national talking point and the public seeks vengeance. Yet every day money that the public has been told is earmarked for development in poor countries is misused and wasted, often very cynically so, with few questions asked. Would taxpayers be as gracious about aid being given on their behalf if they knew that some of that money was being used to exploit developing nations, or to consolidate the power base of some corrupt ruling elites within developing nations?

The exploitation of developing countries, especially those in Africa, is a sensitive issue with many shameful historical overtones. The great empires of the old world stripped Africa of natural resources and human resources in much less enlightened times. If any of the former colonial powers were, today, to mobilise great armies with a view to enslaving and exploiting huge portions of Africa, there would be an international outcry. Most likely, there would be international military action to halt and repel the invaders. Such overt exploitation would simply not be tolerated. However, exploitation of developing nations is taking place today and it is every bit as reprehensible – perhaps even more so given that it is being conducted under the guise of development aid.

This book will look at the effectiveness and ethics of development aid in its current form by questioning the role that aid plays in the world today. What if the reality is that aid promotes relationships of political and economic dependence, of poor countries on rich countries? What if the reality is that aid has historically been used, and continues to be used, to promote the interests of Multinational Corporations, rich country banks and the global capitalist elite, above those of poor people in underdeveloped countries? What if the reality is that aid has facilitated the radical restructuring of the world economy in such a way as to increase the flow of resources from the Global South to the Global North? Would we still be calling for dramatic increases in aid if we knew this was the case? Or would we, on the other hand, be calling for new thinking and new strategies for enabling poor people in poor countries to escape from poverty. This book will argue that this dark alternative scenario is closer to the reality than we as generous, responsible individuals and nations would care to admit.

We have been living in the era of 'aid optimism' when Official Development Assistance (ODA) has increased year on year, and by hugely significant amounts. The United States quadrupled ODA to Africa from $1.4 billion to $5.6 billion a year between 2001 and 2006.[6] Globally, ODA, excluding debt relief and controlling for inflation, grew by $15 billion between 2000 and 2007.[7] The DAC has reported that net ODA for 2008 was $119.8 billion.[8] This compares to the, although large in absolute terms, relatively small amount that was given by donor states to NGDOs in 2004, of $4 billion. Emergency aid only accounts for around 10 per cent of

6. Glennie, 2008:13
7. ibid.:12
8. OECD, 2009. This figure is inflated due to its inclusion of debt relief in calculating development aid.

total aid flows.[9] These last two sets of figures are at the heart of the problem – combined they account for less than 15% of the total ODA. The effectiveness of the rest of this cash is open to question. There are serious questions to be answered concerning its benefit to developing nations. There are also questions around whether it is actually being used to cause great harm to those nations.

NGDOs work at grassroots level. They are on the ground in developing countries, working in and with communities. Often they are the facilitators who enable local voices to be heard, facilitating local priorities to be addressed. That these organisations rely on less than 5% of the total ODA leaves some very serious questions to be answered. The delivery of aid in the form of emergency funding following a disaster is normally spent differently. The provision of water, food, medicine and shelter are entirely altruistic acts on the part of rich nation governments, and so emergency aid can be classified as good aid. Between them NDGOs and emergency aid account for around 15% of aid. That leaves about 85% of ODA, a hugely significant proportion of a large budget, channelled into other schemes. Many of these serve to damage the very countries and peoples that they purport to help.

Aid has harmed the poor for generations and must be seen for what it often is: an aid to political and economic dominance of poor countries by rich countries. It is very difficult for NGDOs to stand up and say such things, which is why they so often fail to criticise the global aid system. There is a culture of not wanting to bite the hand that feeds them, even if that means ignoring some ethically dubious realities. Most Northern NGDOs rely on developed country state funding to finance a large part of their activities. This funding is drawn from the overseas aid budgets of their host countries, so they have a direct interest in preventing the rationale for developed country aid budgets from being undermined. Simply put, increases in overseas aid budgets often lead to increases in charities' income. However, it is the responsibility of every organisation and individual to stand up for the interests of those that they seek to serve, who are the poorest people in the world,

9. Glennie 2008:15-16

including the more than one billion people who live on less than $1 a day. If the structure of global aid is making the poor even poorer, it is the responsibility of those concerned with justice to challenge the *status quo*.

The following chapter summaries provide a brief synopsis of the contents and argument of each of the chapters that follow
.

Chapter 2: Global Poverty and Inequality

Aid is officially sent to developing nations to address the chronic global poverty and inequality that exists in the twenty-first century. In order to understand how effective aid is (or isn't), it's important first to get idea of the extent and urgency of this global crisis. Once the range and extent of global poverty has been established it is easier to judge how effective the current models for aid distribution actually are. It is in this context that criticism of aid that is addressed in the rest of the book will be judged. How poverty rates and the degree of inequality have changed over recent decades is also outlined in this chapter, providing a perspective through which we can judge the effectiveness of increases in ODA. With historically high levels of ODA we would expect a correspondingly big reduction in poverty and inequality, but that does not appear to be the case. The rest of the book considers why ODA is failing to reduce poverty and inequality.

Chapter 3: The Donors

Who are the donors? How much aid do they give? To whom do they give aid? What is their motivation for giving aid to particular countries? These questions are the subject matter of chapter 3. There is an introduction to the main multilateral institutions, looking at their roles, their purpose, their aims, who controls them, and how they operate. Consideration is also given to the bilateral aid that is provided by the US and UK, and the role European Development Banks play in the bilateral aid system. The motivation of donors is explored: are they geared towards promoting commercial and political interests or are they champions of the poor?

Chapter 4: The Recipients
Who are the recipients of ODA? Why do underdeveloped countries accept aid if it often fails to benefit them? A large part of the answer lies the interests and motivations of governments in poor countries. Where political elitism exists the interests of the poor are often compromised in favour of the powerful. Aid can undermine the accountability of governments to their citizens. It can support corruption. Where its application promotes a political system based on patronage and clientalism, it often weakens the institutions of underdeveloped states. Aid can create dependency. Dependency is a trap from which it is very difficult to escape.

Chapter 5: A History of Aid
The history of ODA – from its inception after World War II, up to the present 'new optimism' for aid, is an interesting story. What many think of as benevolence can be seen in a different light. Aid has been and is used to further an imperialist agenda – one that seeks to structure underdeveloped states in such a way as to benefit wealthy capitalist states, and their elites – the context and the methods of this exploitation may have changed over time but the devastation and poverty caused remains the same. Aid has played a central role in exercising political control of poor states as part of the geopolitical logic of the Cold War. As a result Aid has often been used to support brutal dictators who would support the West in the Cold War and implement right wing policies. Aid has always had a political agenda. Conditions attached to loans since the early 1980s have served to restructure underdeveloped states' economies along neoliberal lines, in order to benefit rich countries and capitalist elites.

Chapter 6: Aid, the Neoliberal Policy Agenda, and the Creation of Poverty
This chapter will explore the mechanisms by which the neoliberal policy agenda has promoted the interests of capital, including Multi National Corporations and financial investors, at the expense of the poor. There is ample evidence that aid has been used as a political tool to give these outside interests control over the policies of

underdeveloped countries. The conditions attached to the granting of aid are significant instruments by which this agenda has been forced on poorer countries. Privatisation has played its role as have cuts in social spending. Export orientation and declining terms of trade, financial deregulation and consequent financial crises, and the monetarist/low inflation policies of central banks, have conspired to affect the poor. Even in negotiating International Trade Agreements, aid has been used as leverage to situations that benefit Multinationals at the expense of the world's poor.

Chapter 7: The Macroeconomic Effects of Aid
Aid optimists believe that economic growth benefits the poor. The evidence points in a different direction. The causal relationship between aid and economic growth, as suggested by many aid donors, and accepted by the public, will be questioned. It is evident that the poor have benefited less and less from the growth which has taken place in the context of the economic policies of the past thirty years. This chapter will also outline the role that aid can play in creating currency appreciation, which in turn can harm exports and ultimately undermine the livelihoods of the poor living in underdeveloped countries.

Chapter 8: Recommendations for meaningful change
What can be done to address the problems raised in this book? That's the burning question and the reason for this exploration. A radical break from the current system of aid is called for. It's time to put forward recommendations for new forms of development finance and other policies which could benefit the poor in the Global South. There is urgency to all of this if the chronic emergency of global poverty is to be seriously addressed. The chapter argues that those who seek to promote the interests of the poor must challenge an aid system that undermines improvements in the lives of the poor in the Global South. It also puts forward concrete alternatives that all those who advocate for the poor should be supporting – alternatives that could reverse the negative effects that aid has played in the world for more than sixty years.

CHAPTER 2

Global Poverty and Inequality

Introduction

Aid has been presented to the public as the solution to global poverty. More than that, aid has been presented as the only solution to global poverty. It is comforting to the public when summits such as the G8 at Gleneagles result in massive increases in aid. We are all too familiar with images of ill, impoverished or starving children living in the world's poorest countries. The emotions that such images evoke stir up feelings of pity and anger. We know what the problem is and we want to resolve it. There's a certain comfort, therefore, when our leaders present us with an 'easy' solution in the form of aid. We feel something is being done, but the reality is far less comforting.

It is important to understand the extent and nature of global poverty at the beginning of the twenty-first century in order to appreciate the urgent need for policies that will successfully reduce it. Beyond that, it is also necessary to understand the trends that have taken place in global poverty and inequality. Without that information it would be impossible to assess the extent to which ODA may have had an effect, one way or the other.

The United Nations Development Programme (UNDP) compiles and publishes statistics on human development. They are the primary source of data used in this chapter. Needless to say, the UNDP statistics are subject to some controversy. Therefore, in the interests of balance, where controversy arises, both sides of the argument will be considered.

It will be important also to consider inequality and the changes in inequality that have taken place, both within and between countries. Poverty in the world increasingly affects rural females. Where it occurs in urban areas it is associated with slum dwelling. It will be important also to pay attention to these issues. Sometimes the debate over aid, its extent and its effectiveness can overlook the main issue – namely, the bondage of poverty and its effects: physical, mental, social, economic and spiritual. This brief chapter cannot possibly hope to detail all of the effects of poverty, but it will briefly explore ill health, hunger, educational disadvantage and the devastating effects of poverty on those who are trapped.

Statistics on Global Poverty
In 2007, the United Nations Development Programme (UNDP) estimated that, globally, 1 billion people lived on $1 a day or less, at Purchasing Power Parity (PPP). As PPP takes into account factors such as the cost of living and inflation, it is considered by many a more useful measure than Gross Domestic Product (GDP), or *per capita* income when comparing the standard of living between countries. There is a case to be made for its usefulness, but it's important to recognise that it's not without its drawbacks. The UNDP also estimated that an additional 2.6 billion people, who make up 40% of the world's population, had an income of less than $2 a day.[1] The World Bank defines those living on between $1 and $2 a day as the 'moderately poor'.[2] The $1 a day poverty line is often used to classify those living in extreme poverty, although the World Bank defines those in extreme poverty as those whose income is less than $275 per annum, at PPP.[3]

According to the UNDP, the percentage of the world's population living on less than $1 a day fell from 29% in 1990, to 18% in 2004.[4] The UNDP further estimated that the numbers living in extreme poverty had fallen by 135 million between 1999 and 2004.[5] That would make it seem like there is much to celebrate. However, much of this perceived reduction in extreme poverty was accounted for by the rapid economic growth of China and India, and therefore the extent of this reduction has been called into question. The Asian Development Bank (ADB) produced a report in the same year,

1. UNDP, 2007:25
2. Sachs, 2005:20
3. Spicker *et al*, 2006:75
4. UNDP, 2007:24
5. Ibid

2007, that suggested that absolute poverty in China and India had been dramatically underestimated by the UNDP.

Defining poverty based solely on the vagaries of statistics is at best unhelpful, and at worst cynical. At times the message being supported by the statistics is in such opposition to the reality of poverty on the ground that the message looks confused and ridiculous – if it looks like a duck, sounds like a duck and acts like a duck, then a carefully crafted mean distribution curve isn't going to get you to believe that it is an elephant. In a similar way, those of us who work on the ground recognise extreme poverty. It simply can't be explained away or masked by numbers.

What is in no doubt, regardless of who assesses it, is that absolute poverty in sub-Saharan Africa is increasing, and has been for some time. The numbers of extreme poor in sub-Saharan Africa were estimated to be 150 million in 1981, by the Organisation for Economic Co-Operation and Development (OECD).[6] In 2001, it estimated that the number had increased to just over 300 million. This accounts for almost half the population of sub-Saharan Africa. A further 30% of the population live on between $1 and $2 dollars a day, according to this organisation. Sub-Saharan Africa has the highest rate of extreme and moderate poverty in the world.

South Asia (India accounting for the majority of this population) has the highest absolute numbers living in extreme or moderate poverty, according to the OECD, with more than 400 million people living in extreme poverty and around 650 million people living in moderate poverty.[7] The organisation estimates that around 10 per cent of the population of Latin America lives in extreme poverty (below $1 a day), and a further 15 per cent live in moderate poverty (between $1 and $2 a day). These figures remained fairly constant in Latin America from 1981 to 2001[8] and include more than 100 million people, according to the OECD.[9]

---

6. Sachs, 2005:20-25

7. Ibid

8. This is a perfect example of how figures can be confusing. In fact, the percentage of the population in Latin America who are extremely poor is estimated to have decreased slightly but the absolute numbers are estimated to have increased slightly.

9. Sachs, 2005:20-25

Controversies Surrounding these Estimates

The Asian Development Bank report (2007), 'Purchasing Power Parity: Preliminary Report', calculated income on a PPP basis, and estimated that in 2007, 300 million people in China lived on less than $1 a day. This was three times the estimate that organisations such as the OECD, UNDP and World Bank had previously made. The Asian Development Bank report figures are hardly surprising when we consider that in China the average income on farms, where more than half the population live, is less than $1 a day. What is surprising is the huge difference in the number of people living on less than $1 per day as assessed by these different organisations. With many countries using figures from these organisations when they decide on the level of aid that they give to a region or nation, the reliability or otherwise of these figures has massive policy implications. It is imperative that accurate figures are available. Furthermore, the Asian Development Bank report estimated that in India, 800 million people lived on less than $1 a day, when calculating income in the same way. This was twice the figure that the other organisations had estimated.[10] Since these statistics were produced, it has been estimated that the global food price crisis of 2008 forced an additional 100 million people into extreme poverty.[11]

It is important to note that using the standard benchmark of $1 a day and $2 a day risks greatly underestimating the true extent of global poverty. How could someone living on $3, $4 or $5 a day be classified as anything other than poor? Who decides the $1 and $2 a day threshold and what is their justification for setting poverty at this level? Lorna Gold has argued that using this standard benchmark often greatly understates poverty in higher cost locations in underdeveloped countries.[12] She also notes that analysis of the type of life a person can live on $1 a day has not been widely conducted. According to Gold, it is likely that if this was assessed, the benchmark of extreme poverty would be increased from $1 a day to a higher level, and many more people would come to be defined as extremely poor. It has been argued that such analysis

10. ADB, 2007, in Lines, 2008:24
11. UNDP, 2008:6
12. Gold 2005:27

has not taken place because the outcome would force developed countries to recognise that major changes in the global distribution of wealth would be required to end global poverty. The argument suggests that this would implicate developed countries as responsible for the failure to end global poverty, which is an accusation that they seek to avoid.[13]

Manipulation of statistics to achieve a desired result is an old political trick. In 1930s Germany the number of unemployed was more than halved overnight by the Nazi party – they made it illegal to employ Marxists, Socialists, Jews, pacifists and a number of other social and religious groups, which meant that they no longer counted in the official unemployment figures. Indeed, in my own area of work, leprosy, I am all too conscious that a country which prevents programmes to detect new cases can easily return a statistic showing a decline in incidence. Statistics must be treated with care.

Authors Pogge and Reddy[14] argue along similar lines, that the method for calculating PPP dollars results in an unrealistic assessment of extreme poverty. The PPP method for comparing the cost of living in different countries uses a combination of internationally traded and internationally non-traded goods to compare prices. They argue that poor people's consumption basket contains primarily internationally non-traded goods, and that these are relatively much more expensive than internationally traded goods in poor countries. They also observe that poor people tend to pay a much higher price for basic food stuffs, in poor countries, than the rich do in those countries. As a result of this they argue that the $1 a day at PPP calculation is too low to estimate extreme poverty in the world. They suggest that the World Bank estimates of global poverty (which are broadly similar to the UNDP and OECD estimates) underestimate extreme poverty around the world by as much as 30 per cent.

It is probably the case that an increasing total number of people around the world live above the $1 a day poverty line. According

---

13. Pronk, 2003, in Gold, 2005:30-31
14. 2002, in Kaplinsky, 2005:36-37

to the World Bank, 864 million more people lived above the $1 a day poverty line in 2000 than in 1990.[15] It is difficult to reach a solid conclusion about trends in the overall number living in extreme poverty, other than to say that extreme poverty has been increasing rapidly in sub-Saharan Africa, and that it is increasing at a much slower rate in Eastern Europe, Central Asia, Latin America and the Caribbean.[16] It is possible to conclude that, excluding China, the total number living under the $1 a day rate has increased around the world.[17] It is probably the case that extreme poverty in China has decreased nowhere near as much as has been estimated by the UNDP, World Bank and OECD, in which case the total number of people living in extreme poverty in the world has either remained stable or quite possibly increased since the early 1980s. Either way, there has been no decrease in the numbers of people living in poverty.

Global Inequality
UNDP publishes an Index known as the Human Development Index. This index is produced from a composite measurement that takes into account average life expectancy at birth, GDP *per capita* and average levels of educational attainment. Thomas Lines[18] has studied this data. By analysing those countries classified as High Human Development (about 20% of the world's population – developed countries) and Low Human Development (about 9% of the world's population – developing countries) he noted that average incomes in 2004 were 67 times higher in High HDI countries, i.e. $26,999 *per capita* as opposed to $402 *per capita*. Even if this is converted to equal buying power using PPP, average incomes in High Human Development countries are 24 times higher than those in Low Human Development countries.[19]

Inequality is not only restricted to geographical or regional considerations. In addition to extreme regional inequality, the

---

15. Kaplinsky, 2005:31
16. Sachs, 2005:21
17. Kaplinsky, 2005:31-33
18. Lines 2008:9-14
19. Ibid

inequality between the world's capitalist elite and the poorest people in the world is remarkable. In 1996 the net wealth of the richest 358 people in the world was equal to the total income of the poorest 45% of the world's population. In other words, 358 people had as much wealth between them as 2.3 billion people. Even more remarkably, the richest three individual billionaires in the world, by 1998, owned assets with a greater value than the combined GNP of all Least Developed Countries, with a population of 600 million.[20] These very stark contrasts highlight just how breathtakingly large inequality can be. That 358 people have as much as 2.3 billion people is incredulous enough, but that organisations can go out of their way to try to pretend that many of those 2.3 billion are not poor by setting the threshold for poverty too low, simply stretches all reason and morality to the point of breaking.

Intra-Country Inequality
Most studies of inequality within countries have shown an increase in the period from 1980 to present. This period is particularly relevant to the discussion provided later in this book[21] (Chapter 6 in particular). It would be reasonable to expect that ODA would have functioned as a vehicle to reduce poverty and inequality in that. Regrettably, the evidence points to an increase in both poverty and inequality where ODA has sought to liberalise countries' economies. It would appear that ODA has tended to increase poverty and inequality in those countries. High levels of intra-country inequality have been shown to be associated with high rates of poverty, slower economic growth (because lack of purchasing power constrains domestic demand) and higher levels of unemployment.[22] For these reasons, reducing inequality should be a target or a condition of ODA given to poor countries. Unfortunately the reality (as Chapter 6 discusses) has been the opposite. This raises serious questions on the effectiveness of ODA in recent decades, and indicates that a different approach must be found as a matter of urgency.

20. Harvey, 2005:34-35
21. Chapter 6 in particular
22. Wade, 2008: 422

A study[23] of 73 countries from the post World War II period to the present, covering 80% of the world's population, found that in the majority of countries inequality fell gradually from the 1950s to the 1970s, before increasing markedly in the period from 1980 to the present. Interestingly, it is this period from 1980 to present that is synonymous with ODA being used as an instrument to promote Neoliberal economic policies in poor countries ... but more of that in chapter 6.

It has been noted that, in a global context, China has experienced the most dramatic change in income distribution.[24] Since the mid-1980s, as China has become increasingly integrated into the global economy, as it adopts more and more free market characteristics, sharp rises in inequality have emerged. UNICEF has provided data that shows that in China, the poorest 40% of households receive only 16% of total household incomes, and that the richest 20% of households control 48% of total household income.[25] Inequality, since the early 1980s in China, has increased sharply between urban and rural areas, coastal and interior areas, and within urban and rural areas.[26] This has resulted in a crisis in rural livelihoods in China. A knock-on effect is seen in the mass migration from rural to urban areas and an explosion in the urban slum-dwelling population.

Inter-Country Inequality
ODA has been instrumental in restructuring the world economy in such a way as to promote the transfer of wealth from poor to rich countries. This may not be a popular assertion to make but a close analysis of the available data suggests that it is a factual claim. Kaplinsky[27] has shown that when weighted for population size, an international comparison of *per capita* income reveals that global inequality actually decreased from 1980 to 1998. This, on the surface looks like a victory and improvement, but beneath the

23. See Kaplinsky 2005:41
24. Kaplinsky (2005:43)
25. UNICEF 2009 online
26. Kaplinsky ibid
27. Ibid

headline lies another story. The spectacular growth of China has distorted the picture. The Chinese economy grew by an annualised rate of 10% throughout the 1980s and 1990s. This led to a rapid increase in *per capita* income in China. Since China has 20% of the world's population it is not surprising that global *per capita* incomes have become more equal.[28] We have, however, already noted that the income distribution in China has rapidly become more unequal during this time. Therefore, the rise in *per capita* income in China and its effect on increasing global inter-country *per capita* income equality does not reflect increasing global equality in incomes, but rather the opposite. In short, over the period studied by Kaplinsky, a relatively small number of people in China became very rich, with little, if any, increase in the number of people living above the poverty line in the country. The increase in wealth of China as a nation is accounted for, and held by, a small number of individuals. If we exclude this elite group from the figures then poverty in China has increased from 1980 to 1998.

Kaplinsky's observation is worth noting: when China is left out of the equation, global inequality in *per capita* incomes has increased markedly since the early 1980s, with poor countries receiving an increasingly small share of global incomes. Wade[29] has provided data illustrating that the *per capita* Gross National Product (GNP) of several poor regions has been falling, as a proportion of the GNP of industrialised countries, for some time. This has been the case in Sub-Saharan Africa where this proportion was just 2% in 1999, half what it was in 1980. It has also fallen in West Asia, North Africa and Latin America as well, and it remained static in South Asia. Only the East Asian economies have gained an increasing share of the global proportion to GNP.[30]

Overall, when we take together the changing pattern of global inequality within and between countries, it is clear that the world has become a more unequal place since the early 1980s. The poorest 20% of the world's population received 2.3% of global income in 1960. By 1991, they received just 1.4% of global income and by

28. ibid
29. Wade 2008: 413
30. ibid

2000 they received just 1.1%.[31] ODA has played a significant role in facilitating this change in the distribution of incomes in the world, again providing testimony that a new approach to aid is imperative.

Rural Poverty

The figures in Lines' work on the Human Development Index, mentioned above, show that of the Low Human Development countries for which data is available, 18 were dependent on exporting commodities (raw materials or unprocessed food crops) and only 6 were not, in 2003-2005. As shall be outlined in Chapter 6, declining terms of trade for commodities, in the context of forced liberalisation facilitated by ODA, have been a major source of increasing poverty for these countries. These figures also suggest that the poorest countries, with the highest levels of poverty, are often economically dependent on agriculture. There is a crisis in rural livelihoods in underdeveloped countries.

According to the International Fund for Agricultural Development (IFAD),[32] three quarters of the world's extreme poor (those on less than $1 a day), live in rural areas. IFAD has also highlighted that the poorest of the rural poor live in remote areas, and 634 million of them live on marginal lands. Many of the rural poor are smallholder farmers with a few acres or hectares at most. Many are subsistence or near subsistence farmers, growing most or all of the food that their household consumes, and therefore they are not as reliant on cash income as the landless poor. It has been estimated that around half of the world's hungry people are smallholder farmers. It has also been estimated that 20% of the world's hungry are rural landless, and a further 10% depend on herding, fishing or forest resources. Only 20% of the world's hungry people live in urban areas .[33] From this it's obvious that hunger, as well as poverty, are concentrated in rural areas in underdeveloped countries.

31. Gersham and Irwan, 2000: 14
32. IFAD, 2001, in, Lines, 2008:6
33. Lines, 2008:7

Global Slums

This crisis in rural livelihoods has led to mass migration to cities by the rural poor, in a desperate search for a means to survive. Slums in underdeveloped countries grew from having an aggregate population of 654 million in 1990, to 933 million in 2005, and are home to one in three of those who live in cities in underdeveloped countries.[34] Slums are defined as conditions in which at least one of the four basic requirements for a living space is absent: sanitation facilities, water facilities, durable housing or sufficient living area.[35]

In India alone the population living in slums stands at 158.4 million. The slum dwelling population in India is increasing at a rate 250% faster than the total population is growing. In China 193.8 million people live in slums, which is over a third of the urban population in the countryside.[36] Official estimates put the number of rural to urban migrants currently living in China at 114 million, making it the largest mass migration in human history. To put this in context, the entire Irish migration to America from 1820 to 1930 was thought to have involved 4.5 million people.[37] The majority of these migrants are women and they make up the majority of slum dwellers in China.[38] In China, as with slum formation around the world, this has largely been driven by a crisis in rural livelihoods. Africa's slums are growing at twice the speed of its cities, which are undergoing a 'population explosion'.[39] Taken together, these statistics indicate an unprecedented explosion in urban poverty around the world.

Gender and Poverty

The 1995 UNDP Human Development Report was devoted to the topic of gender inequality. It estimated that 70 per cent of people living in extreme poverty in the world are women or girls. It also

---

34. UN-HABITAT, 2006:16 and UNDP, 2008:43
35. UNDP, 2008:43
36. Davis, 2006:4-18
37. Ibid
38. Harvey, 2005:127
39. Davis, 2006:4-18

noted that the number of rural women living in poverty rose by 50 per cent from 1975-1995. Women receive a much lower wage than men, as a result of working more often in the informal economy, working more often in lower paid jobs, or receiving less pay for equal work. Globally, women received only 26 per cent of total income from work in 1994. The report further noted that women are more likely to be unemployed than men in all regions in the world. Women receive far less credit from lending institutions than men since they are assessed more often than their male counterparts as having no collateral. This is often the result of formal titles to landholdings being held by men rather than women and makes it more difficult for women to escape from poverty than men. The report compared women and men's achievements in the Human Development Index (HDI) and found that in all regions of the world women fare worse than men according to this measure. The consequences of this were most severe in the poorest countries, in which a low attainment in the HDI exists in the general population, since the attainment in these countries is lower still for women.

ODA should aim to redress the imbalance between men and women. However, Structural Adjustment Policies (SAPs), imposed on poor countries as a condition for receipt of ODA have been widely observed to have increased female poverty and hardship in poor countries. Again, this is something to be explored in Chapter 6. One aspect of these policies has been to dramatically cut social provision in poor countries, resulting in reduced provision of water, healthcare, electricity, education and other basic services. Women have absorbed a disproportionate amount of the impact of the cuts in services. This is because women more often than men are responsible for providing domestic labour, and these services often provide support to this type of work.[40] The social costs of service cuts as a consequence of SAPs fell more heavily on women than on men, in poor countries.

---

40. Razavi, 1999:478

Outcomes of Poverty: Ill Health, Hunger and Educational Disadvantage
Ill health and premature mortality is closely associated with
poverty. In 2000, more than 11 million children died before their
fifth birthday. Just 1% of those eleven million deaths occurred in a
rich country.[41] To make sense of and absorb the enormity of this
statistic, let's think about it in another way: if the 99% had not
lived in poverty we could reasonably expect that around 100,000
would still have died, but almost eleven million would have sur-
vived – a complete reversal of fortunes. It is known that the main
causes of under-five mortality are pneumonia, malaria, diarrhoea
and measles, which are all easily treatable through proven inter-
ventions and simple improvements in basic health systems.[42] The
inability of poor people to access basic healthcare services is a
major negative outcome of poverty, and one that ought to be easily
addressed through more effective targeting of ODA.

About a third of those who die in infancy, i.e. 3.66 million,
suffer from under-nutrition. In 2004, 140 million of the world's
613 million children were underweight while almost half of the
children in South Asia were underweight. In 1998, 843 million
people were classified as undernourished, on the basis of their
food intake.[43] In 2003, one in four people in South Asia were
chronically undernourished (303 million), while one in three people
in sub-Saharan Africa were likewise chronically undernourished
(194 million). As we have seen, the majority of these people are
the rural poor in underdeveloped countries. Under-nutrition is
another major negative outcome of poverty in poor countries.

The poor are particularly disadvantaged in terms of educational
attainment in underdeveloped countries.[44] The UNDP has calculated that 84% of children in urban areas in countries that they classify
as 'developing' attend primary school, but that just 74% of children in
rural areas do so. Poverty has also been shown to be a major determin-
ant of lack of access to primary level education for children. Surveys
in sub-Saharan Africa have revealed that children from the poorest

41. World Bank, 2004:1
42. UNDP, 2008:21
43. World Bank: 2004: 1
44. 2008:13

households are the least likely to attend primary school, regardless of whether they are from rural or urban areas.[45] The fact that fewer children from rural areas attend primary school in poor countries is therefore a reflection of higher rural poverty rates. Girls are also disadvantaged relative to boys in access to primary education. In 2006, 100 boys were enrolled in primary school per 94 girls, in poor countries.[46] The disadvantage experienced by girls in access to primary education is due to the interaction of poverty with the culturally embedded domination of women by men around the world, which tends to result in girls and women being 'the poorest of the poor', as observed already in this chapter.

Conclusion

Conventional estimates, which point to declining numbers of people living in extreme poverty throughout the world, underestimate the extent of global poverty. Estimates of global poverty vary widely, for all kinds of reasons. Extreme poverty in sub-Saharan Africa is increasing rapidly by any estimate, and is increasing in a number of other regions, regardless of the estimate used. Increasing inequality between the richest and the poorest in the world has also been outlined, in particular in the period from around 1980. The fact that poverty more often than not has a rural and female face in underdeveloped countries is also well established. The most negative aspects associated with poverty – hunger, ill health and educational disadvantage – have all increased from 1980, coninciding with increases in ODA. The role played by aid in allowing this global crisis of poverty to develop, and more often than not, encouraging its perpetration, needs to be investigated, and radical new thinking is required if poverty is ever going to be eliminated.

45. Ibid
46. Ibid

CHAPTER 3

The Donors

There are a number of questions that need to be explored to fully understand the complexities of aid, its donation and the evaluation of its effectiveness. It is not enough to answer these questions in a superficial way, as has often been the case, nor is it acceptable to simply turn a blind eye to the answers when they do not fit in with the romantic view that we have of aid. The questions themselves are quite straightforward. What exactly is Official Development Assistance (ODA)? Who is giving it, and to whom? And how much is being given? The answer to these questions will help in understanding how aid is channelled to underdeveloped countries – mainly as bilateral (government to government) or multilateral (international agency to government) aid. The roles played by the major multilateral institutions need also to be explored. This chapter will ask those questions.

After that, attention will turn to the *modus operandi* of the largest bilateral donor: the United States (US), and a smaller donor: the United Kingdom (UK). Their policies and practices will be discussed and contrasted. The role played by European Development Banks in the business of bilateral aid will also be considered, before concluding with a discussion of the Paris Declaration on Aid Effectiveness (PDAE) and the Accra Action Agenda (AAA) – two major international agreements that have in recent years helped to structure the relationships between aid recipients and donors. The extent to which the commercial and geopolitical self interests of donors dominates in the international aid system ought also to be given some consideration.

To answer the first set of questions requires examination of the role of the Development Assistance Committee (DAC) of the Organisation for Economic Cooperation and Development (OECD). The OECD was established after the Second World War

(WWII) to administer the US Marshall Plan for the reconstruction of Europe.[1] Since then it has evolved into a grouping of 23 of the richest states. That group promotes free market and other neo-liberal economic policies around the world. These policies have been championed with the zeal of religious dogma and very little consideration has been given to how appropriate the policies actually are for individual nations. The DAC coordinates the relationship between the OECD and underdeveloped countries; in particular, it plays a part in determining the strategies that the donor states adopt, setting standards for 'best practice' and peer review mechanisms. One of the significant roles played by the DAC is in determining which categories of financial flows should be considered as Official Development Assistance and which should not.

Since ODA from OECD countries makes up the bulk of international aid flows, the DAC's role in determining what is and is not considered to be ODA is very significant. DAC members are keen for financial flows from their governments to be counted as ODA, since public opinion in developed countries generally supports the allocation of aid to the developing world. In popular media discourse and among the public in general, aid is seen as a symbol of the generosity of donor states and their populations. It can also be viewed as a status symbol, with a high level of ODA acting as an indication of the wealth of a nation. The public in donor countries overwhelmingly back the aid-giving activities of their governments, and donating aid is often supported by the media and celebrities. Public opinion in the United States represents an important exception to this rule, where there is little public support for overseas aid programmes.[2] In large part as a result of advocacy from NGOs, the percentage of Gross National Income (GNI) that is categorised as ODA matters when governments face their electorate at the ballot box. It is a popular move on humanitarian grounds but it is also shows the voting public that the economy is in good health. In short, it matters greatly to the governments of donor states how the DAC classifies particular sorts of financial flows. The pressure from donor governments to classify all kinds

---

1. Tandon 2008:106-107
2. Chhotray and Hulme, 2009: 38, Boas and McNeill, 2003: 23-25

of assistance as ODA has played a major part in tricking the public
into believing that the aid efforts of their governments, carried out
on their behalf, is doing tremendous amounts of good around the
world. The semantics of classification hides the terrible truth –
most ODA is adding to the problem of poverty.

According to the DAC, ODA is defined as assistance to countries and territories on the DAC List of ODA Recipients and to
multilateral development institutions which is:[3]

provided by official agencies, including state and local governments, or by their executing agencies.

each transaction of which is administered with the objective of
promoting economic development and welfare of developing
countries; and

concessional and has a grant element of at least 25% (calculated at a discount rate of 10%).

The DAC also includes debt restructuring for underdeveloped
countries; interest subsidies; spending on promoting 'development awareness', and administrative costs, as categories of ODA.[4]
To exemplify the absurdity of this system, imagine if a developing
country owes a developed country $10 billion. The developed
country agrees to some small change in the terms of the loan – a
lower interest rate or an extension to the loan term. This can,
according to the classification, be regarded as $10 billion of new
ODA, even though the developing country has not handed over
one dollar of new money. Official Equity Investments (OEIs) by
DAC members in underdeveloped countries are also considered
to count as ODA, since they are considered to have a development
oriented intention.[5]

The DAC categorises aid into that which is broadly bilateral
(government to government) and that which is broadly multilateral
(provided by donors to the multilateral institutions including the
World Bank, IMF, Regional Development Banks and UN agencies).
For ODA to be considered as multilateral, pooled contributions

3. DAC, 2009: 48
4. Ibid
5. Tandon, 2008:6

must lose their identity as originating from a particular donor state (be no longer administered by the donor government or a domestic agency of the donor state) and become an integral part of the financial assets of the multilateral institution in question.[6] The reality is that the smaller contributors to the multilateral agencies have little or no input into how these organisations deliver aid. With this loss of oversight comes a loss of accountability – the donor can boast a generous ODA level but they cannot always testify to how the aid has been spent, or what detrimental conditions have been imposed on any recipient of that aid. It is simply not good enough for a country to hand over huge amounts of money and then take themselves out of the distribution process, claiming ignorance if that aid is used nefariously. Pleading ignorance in this way would not be accepted in any other area of public spending. One can imagine the outcry if billions of expenditure on the health service could not be accounted for. How much more intense would that criticism be if it was discovered that the money was being spent on things that actually damaged the health of the public?

Yash Tandon has provided a critique of this, universally quoted and legitimised, definition of aid.[7] Central to this critique are observations that he has made about how ODA is defined. He considers the criteria for ODA that financial flows should have a grant element of 25 per cent and be calculated against a notional interest rate of 10 per cent. He observes that this definition was arrived at in the 1970s, when interest rates were high. In the interim interest rates have been reduced greatly across a number of years, in most OECD countries (and are almost zero today). This, he observes, has made it much easier for DAC members to make up the 25 per cent grant element of loans. He further observes that much ODA is officially 'tied' to the purchase of goods or services from the donor state, and that according to the UN this practice increases costs by 25 to 60 per cent. According to Tandon, this additional cost negates the 25 per cent grant element of much ODA.

His critique also highlights that in cases where the grant

6. Ibid
7. Tandon 2008: 4-9

element is 25 per cent, the remaining 75 per cent must eventually be paid back, and therefore ultimately adds to the debt burden of the recipient country. In relation to the inclusion of official equity investments (OEIs) as a category of ODA, Tandon asks rhetorically, 'Has anybody done research into what these OEIs are and whose interests they really serve?'[8] This analysis will return to this question later, highlighting the commercial self interest of donor states in making OEIs, specifically in the case of ODA channelled through European Development Banks. In this critique we can glimpse that ODA, according to the DAC definition, may not be as benevolent as it is popularly held to be. Indeed, it may not even represent a net flow of financial resources from developed to underdeveloped countries, when the effects of tied aid and debt repayments are taken into account.

The DAC provides comprehensive statistics on annual ODA flows and on individual member's contributions to overall ODA. The table opposite is taken from their website, and summarises the magnitude of global ODA from 1990 to 2007, projecting forward hypothetically from 2007 to 2010 (based on the assumption that DAC members will meet their commitment to achieve ODA equalling 0.7 per cent of GNI by 2010). It is the most up to date data that is available.

It is clear from the graph that ODA levels fell off after 1990 and began to pick up again around 2000. It is no coincidence that ODA saw a decline post 1990, the period at the end of the Cold War. As Chapter 5 will illustrate, one of the guiding rationales for providing ODA during the Cold War was to win allies for the West in the geopolitical struggle with the Soviet Union. Once this perceived necessity ceased to exist, with the collapse of the Eastern Bloc, so too did much of the rationale for providing ODA. It's not too big a logical jump to conclude that political interests were behind the pre-1990 ODA expenditure more than humanitarian concern.

The increases in ODA since 2000 correspond to the emerging era of the renewed optimism for aid ushered in by the UN Millennium Summit and the MDGs. This was the period in which

---

8. Ibid: 10

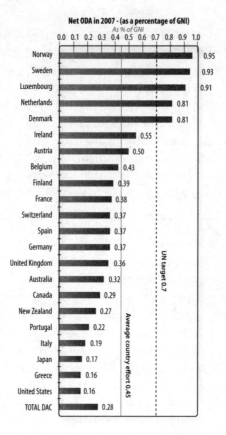

Net ODA in 2007 - (as a percentage of GNI)

Source: OECD, Development Cooperation Report, 2009 (p 104)

donors made grand predictions of the possibility for aid to achieve development targets. This new optimism for aid will be critically discussed in Chapters 5 and 6. It is interesting and worthwhile noting that the only year in which ODA levels have reached 1990 levels, in terms of the percentage of GNI allocated, in recent times, was 2005. The spike in the graph is accounted for by large debt relief deals that were agreed with Iraq and Nigeria in that year.[9] It is also worth noting that ODA to Africa more than doubled between 2000 and 2006. The chapters that follow will discuss some

9. Glennie, 2008:5-6

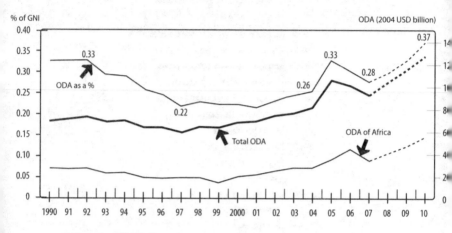

Source: OECD, Development Cooperation Report, 2009 (p 151)

of the implications this has had for African states and their populations, many of which are among the group of Least Developed Countries (LDCs).The table above is also taken from the DAC website, and summarises the origins of global ODA for 2007.

What can be seen instantly, from the preceding charts, is that the US contributes by far the greatest share of ODA of any DAC member state, in absolute terms, but paradoxically contributes the least in terms of the share of GNI contributed toward ODA. The $21.79 billion that the US contributed to ODA in 2007 accounted for more than 20 per cent of the DAC, total of $103.9 billion. This is simply explained by the size of the US economy, which dwarfs all other DAC members' economies, and indeed dwarfs the economies of all other countries in the world. The primary significance of this for the global aid system is that the US exerts a dominant influence on the multilateral institutions that distribute the pooled resources of donors, since voting rights in most of these institutions are proportionate to the funds that member states contribute. The US also exerts a dominant influence on the global bilateral aid system, through its official aid agencies. While donating more in absolute terms, but less in real terms, the US, it can be argued, has a disproportionate voice in the direction and policy of ODA.

When we take an overview of the primary destinations of ODA, it is clear that US foreign policy has a great influence on the overall direction of official aid flows. Iraq received the greatest amount of ODA of any country in 2007, receiving $9 billion, almost 10 per cent of global ODA. Afghanistan received the second largest amount of ODA globally, receiving $3 billion in the same year (OECD, 2009). Of this total, the US provided more than $4 billion in ODA to Iraq in 2007 and almost $1.5 billion to Afghanistan. It hardly needs to be pointed out that both of these countries are currently the subject of US military intervention and are of central geopolitical concern to the US.

As Yash Tandon has written, in the case of these countries, winning the war is not enough, and the 'imperial project', as he terms it, must go further to win the hearts and minds of the people. This project, according to him, involves imbuing the ideologies of globalisation, market fundamentalism, human rights (referring only to civil and political rights rather than including also social and economic rights), and the ideology of liberal democratic governance in these societies, thus 'colonising' the minds of the people, once the military victory is complete. He sees the central function of ODA to these countries as being to support this project. It is certainly a neat trick that is being employed by the US – the US has an obligation in Iraq and Afghanistan to address the poverty which has partly been created by the wars. By redirecting money already earmarked for poverty alleviation to these two countries the US can kill two birds with one stone – namely meeting its aid commitment and addressing the issue of reconstruction in countries where it is warring. It is almost like an individual using money that they have already donated to charity to pay their taxes.

Only a small proportion of overall bilateral ODA is allocated to Non-Governmental Organisations (NGOs). Overall, NGOs are only responsible for distributing 4% of ODA,[10] this despite the fact that in the popular imagination ODA is often associated with being disbursed primarily by these agencies.

---

10. OECD, 2009, online

Multilateralism

Overall, according to the DAC, its members contribute nearly one third of their gross ODA to multilateral institutions. The European Commission is the largest recipient of core funding, receiving 36 per cent of all multilateral contributions. It managed 17.3 per cent of total EU aid in 2006, or $10.2 billion. According to Carbone,[11] a 'high degree of fragmentation has undermined the effectiveness of EU aid and prevented it from influencing the course of international development'.

The World Bank receives 24% of multilateral contributions.[12] Although it receives a smaller proportion of multilateral contributions than the European Commission, its financial weight is far greater. The reason for this is that member states guarantee an amount of 'callable capital'. They guarantee this capital, but do not actually pay it to the bank. This guarantee provides the bank with a very strong credit rating and enables it to raise large amounts of finance at preferential interest rates on international markets. In spite of not receiving the greatest amount of 'paid in' contributions amongst the multilateral institutions, it is able to function as the largest provider of development assistance in the world and is therefore a key player in setting the agenda for global ODA.[13]

The International Monetary Fund (IMF), often considered the twin of the World Bank, is responsible for assisting countries that face a balance of payments crisis, for which it offers loans of foreign currency in return for an agreement to a package of policy changes by the receiving country.[14] The policies pursued by the IMF are critically discussed in Chapter 6. For the moment, it is enough to assert that its power is greatly increased by the fact that many donors make their disbursement of bilateral funds to crisis hit countries dependent upon these recipients making a deal with the IMF.[15] The various United Nations (UN) agencies receive 20% of multilateral contributions.[16] The UN agencies include the

11. 2007:30
12. DAC, 2009: 67-68
13. Boas and McNeill, 2003:17
14. Vreeland, 2003:9
15. Carbone, 2007:63
16. DAC, 2009: 67-68

United Nations Development Programme (UNDP), the United Nations Children's Fund (UNICEF), the World Food Programme (WFP) and the United Nations High Commissioner for Refugees (UNHCR). Later in this chapter an overview of the most influential multilateral institutions will be provided.

The region that received the most ODA in 2007 was sub-Saharan Africa, receiving a total of $34,267 million. South Asia received a total of $12,869 million in the same year.[17] The Middle East received $14,132 million.[18] It is remarkable given that South Asia, which has the largest number of absolutely poor people in the world, received less ODA than the Middle East, with a much lower number of the world's poor living there. One can only conclude that this largely reflects the geopolitical and economic interest that donors (primarily the US) have in the Middle East. Latin America, including South and Central America received a total of $6,839 million in 2007.[19] Countries in the Far East received $7,126 million in that year.[20]

The countries categorised as Least Developed Countries (LDCs), which have the highest rates of extreme poverty, received $32,530 million in ODA in 2007, with other Low Income Countries (LICs) receiving $15,573 million.[21] Lower Middle Income countries received $25,766 million and Upper Middle Income Countries received $4,086 million in the same year.[22] That the group of upper and lower middle income countries, combined, received nearly as much ODA as the group of LDCs, is a further indicator that other concerns exist for donors in allocating ODA, apart from targeting countries with the highest rates of poverty.

The World Bank
The World Bank and IMF were established after WWII. These institutions formed the basis of a new international financial system,

---

17. OECD, 2009:204-207
18. Ibid
19. Ibid
20. Ibid
21. OECD, 2009:207
22. Ibid

created by the capitalist Allied powers, referred to as the Bretton Woods' system. The initial purpose of the World Bank, or International Bank for Reconstruction and Development as it was then known, was to aid the reconstruction of Europe after the war. This was a key foreign policy objective of the US at the time, since an economically strong Europe was needed as a trading partner. It was also considered that the reconstruction of Europe was necessary to provide a bulwark against the emergent, powerful, left wing movements of the time. From the very beginning then, it was clear that the World Bank existed to promote US objectives internationally. The World Bank is owned by its 180 member states, made up of both recipients and donors, but voting rights are based on a 'one dollar one vote' system, in which each member state has voting rights proportionate to the combined amount of 'paid in' and 'callable' capital that it provides.

This fact has given the US considerable leverage over bank policy, as the largest shareholder. The President of the World Bank has always been an American. This, along with the location of the Bank's premises, along with the IMF, in Washington DC, has always facilitated it with a close affinity to US concerns. As outlined in Chapter 5, the US has considered that promoting economic development through the World Bank in geopolitically significant poor countries has been in its national interest.[23] In more recent times the World Bank has promoted neoliberal economic policies. However, these policies further US interests in the Global South and have contributed to the creation of poverty on a global scale.[24]

---

23. Boas and McNeill, 2003:17-28
24. For a description of neoliberal globalisation and a discussion of its impact, see chapter 6. For the moment, it is sufficient to describe this process as the increasingly global promotion of free market economic policies,

The International Monetary Fund (IMF)

The IMF was set up after WWII, in order to promote exchange rate stability by monitoring and managing exchange rates in the global currency market. At the time, and up until 1971, the US dollar was guaranteed at a set rate against US gold reserves. A related function of the IMF was to provide emergency support to countries with short term balance of payments deficits. It uses its vast fund of international currencies and gold to support exchange rates. When the gold standard was removed in 1971, the IMF lost one of its major functions. Since this time it has focused on providing short term support to countries with balance of payment deficits. All of the world's major economies are members of the IMF – more than 180 states in total. Like the World Bank, voting rights are based on the amount of funds that member countries contribute. The funds that member countries contribute also determine the amount of funds that a member can access in times of emergency. The IMF sets a quota for each member, telling them how much they must contribute, based on the size of their economy.

The US is the biggest contributor to the IMF and therefore has the most votes. A consequence of the way that voting rights are determined in the IMF is that when it provides funds to under-developed countries that are in financial crises, it acts as an inter-mediary between the core industrial states in the world and the interests that they represent, on the one hand, and the recipient country on the other.[25] A significant outcome of this is that the IMF can be more interested in protecting the interests of global financial capital rather than those of the poor in countries seeking assist-ance, when it intervenes in economic crises. This point is discussed further in Chapter 6.

The IMF displaces the economic costs of financial crises onto the poor in underdeveloped countries, rather than onto international

---

within which the global free flow of capital is promoted, regulation of capital is removed, secure conditions for capital to operate in are promoted and the market rather than the state is promoted as the means to provid-ing for society in every area of life. This book will argue that neoliberal globalisation is a political project, launched by global elites, to return power and wealth to themselves as a class, on a global scale.

25. Boas and McNeill, 2003:28-35

creditors, or other financial elites. It achieves this through attaching conditions to loans, in which recipient governments must agree to change policies that are perceived as 'bad' by the IMF, to policies that the IMF perceives as 'good'.[26] It is worth noting here that, at certain times and in certain places, governments have brought in the IMF not through necessity in a time of emergency, but in order to provide a 'scapegoat' for making unpopular decisions that deflate the economy and redistribute incomes upwards from the poor to the rich. The political costs associated with rejecting an IMF deal include sending negative signals to creditors and investors along with refusals of bilateral ODA, often in the form of debt rescheduling, from creditor countries. According to Vreeland,[27] the political costs of rejecting an IMF deal often provide enough leverage for a government to introduce policies that benefit domestic elites, but for which they would normally face overwhelming domestic opposition.

The group of multilateral institutions includes the Inter-American Development Bank (IDB), the African Development Bank (AfDB) and the Asian Development Bank (ADB). The impetus for the creation of these banks came partly from post-colonial nationalism in underdeveloped regions, which saw regional co-operation as key to asserting independence, and also, paradoxically, partly from US foreign policy concerns during the Cold War. The Cuban revolution in 1958-59 and the political resentment toward the US in the region at the time led directly to the founding of the first of these: the Inter-American Development Bank. The US, at the time, was keen to avert further revolutions and felt that the promotion of economic development in the region, through this bank, would go some way to preventing them.[28] In the negotiations that led to the founding of the ADB, as a result of ideological Asian Nationalism among the underdeveloped regional states, the US held to the view that it should maintain a majority share in the bank's ownership and electoral system. In the end they did not achieve this and managed to secure only 45 per cent of the voting

26. Vreeland, 2003:11
27. 2003:12-16
28. Boas and McNeill, 2003:36

rights as a bloc.[29] However, when Asian developed countries are included (New Zealand, Australia and Japan), this regional bloc controls 60 per cent of the votes. As a result, although the US is a permanent board member of the bank, it is unlike most other multilateral institutions in being majority Asian controlled. The AfDP was the only regional development bank that was established without donor involvement, but found itself chronically short of funds in the 1960s and 70s.[30] In the early 1980s the bank was forced to permit the involvement of non-regional members. It has been beset by divisions between its regional and non-regional member states which have greatly weakened its influence over time.[31]

The United Nations Development Programme (UNDP)

The UNDP was established in 1956 as an amalgamation of several UN agencies. It is governed by a board which has more represent-atives from underdeveloped than developed regions, on a permanent basis.[32] Voting is on a one member one vote basis, which, uniquely among multilateral institutions, gives under-developed regions majority control over the institution. Unlike the Development Banks and the IMF, it does not provide loans, but instead offers grants and technical assistance. As a result it is in constant need of funding. In addition, it does not control the decisions regarding the allocation of all the funds it secures. Increasingly, donors have earmarked funding to the institution for particular purposes, as they are aware that given free reign the UNDP will not necessarily distribute funds according to devel-oped country priorities. The UNDP has always had difficulty attracting donor funding, primarily because it is not donor controlled. For this reason it has had little influence over the global system of ODA, which has remained dominated by those institu-tions that reflect (or are controlled by) donor interests. This once

29. Ibid: 36-38
30. Ibid
31. Ibid
32. Boas and McNeill, 2003:38-40

again points to the need for control that pervades the thinking of developed nations with regard to aid.

To summarise, the most powerful multilateral aid agencies, i.e. those best equipped to make a real difference in the level of global poverty, are controlled by those donor countries who contribute most to them. The US has the greatest influence by far. It has the greatest say over when and where aid is distributed. It also determines under what terms and conditions that aid is made available. The aid is given in such a way that it compliments US foreign policy, or in some other way serves the interests of the US. Several regional groups have been established in an attempt to reduce the influence of the US and US foreign policy. Wherever this has happened, the US has, over time, always managed, somehow, to exert its influence. The *modus operandi* is to infiltrate the organisation, or put external pressure on the organisation, or isolate the organisation to such an extent that it becomes completely ineffective.

Bilateralism

The major part of ODA is administered bilaterally. Each donor has its own bilateral aid agency, so there are too many to mention here. Since the US is by far the largest (net) donor, USAID is worthy of consideration. DFID, The United Kingdom's agency is worthy of examination since it is a good example of a smaller donor. Several European donors also operate Development Banks, in which ODA is used to co-finance commercial investments in underdeveloped countries (OEIs referred to earlier). The operations of these banks are also noteworthy.

A general shift has taken place in bilateral aid over the last ten years. In the past there was a focus on funding particular projects. Project management units were separate from government. Financial management took place in organisations outside of the recipient government's own budgetary systems. Now there is a focus on direct budget support for the recipient countries' governments. Budget support takes the form of providing financial support for the recurrent costs of government ministries. This might, for example, be the salaries of civil servants or public sector employees such as teachers and nurses. It has increasingly become the norm for donors to support the health and education sectors in this way, in particular.[33] The World Bank and IMF have been providing aid as budget support for some time, but the move by bilateral donors to do this is a more recent phenomenon. The US has tended to focus on providing project support rather than budget support to recipients of ODA. In this respect the US is unusual, and this marks a difference between bilateral aid from European donors and the US.

US Bilateral Aid

Since the US is the single biggest bilateral donor, its bilateral aid agencies are the most significant. Historically and up to present, US foreign aid has always been 'tied' to recipient countries agreeing to promote US commercial interests, by purchasing goods and services from with the US using the ODA that they receive. One estimate has suggested that up to 80 per cent of US aid flows return to the country through purchases of goods and services from US companies.[34] As a result up to 80% of aid actually makes it back to this source. Accordingly US aid primarily supports specific projects rather than sector wide (or government budget support) approaches. The US has a number of bilateral aid agencies, of which USAID is the biggest.[35]

USAID

USAID is the principal bilateral US aid agency, and is subject to the control of the US State Department, the equivalent of the ministry for foreign affairs in other countries.[36] Consequently, the funding priorities of USAID are in line with US strategic, commercial and diplomatic foreign policy priorities. USAID was initially established to separate security based aid and development aid, but in recent years this boundary has become blurred. This is particularly the case with regard to conflict and post-conflict situations

---

33. Ndaruhutse and Brannelly, 2006:9
34. Sogge, 2002:70
35. Chhotray and Hulme, 2009:37-38
36. Chhotray and Hulme, 2009:38

such as Iraq and Afghanistan, the largest recipients of US ODA, where development aid has followed an overtly security related agenda.[37]

Essex[38] notes that 'USAID now makes direct connections between economic liberalisation, development progress, and US national security, with developing states understood as sources of, and focal points for combating, global terrorism.' This view, which dominates in the US, believes 'developing states' 'breed' terrorism. Accordingly international development has taken on a new significance within US foreign policy since the emergence of the 'War on Terror'.[39]

Within an overall ideology that insists that, 'the state's proper role lies in facilitating neoliberal globalisation and ensuring the security of internationalising capital',[40] the US administration ranks states in the Global South according to their 'deservedness' to receive aid. Deservedness, according to this framework, rests on one of two criteria: either that the country in question is willing to become a trading partner to the US and promote US commercial interests by introducing neoliberal policies (economic criteria), and/or that the country in question is strategically significant to the US in geopolitical terms (political/security criteria). Deserving countries are given aid according to these criteria. Aid is withheld from those that do not progress along the path of neoliberal re-form.[41] Withholding aid from countries that do not implement particular policy changes that have been stipulated by the donor is referred to as aid conditionality. These types of conditionalities are intended to push countries along the path to neoliberal economic reform.

According to USAID logic, 'fragile' or 'failed' states are those that do not have political institutions in place to promote economic liberalisation, or that resist it. This is seen as the cause of terrorism-breeding poverty in those states. Aid is used to encourage recipient

---

37. Ibid
38. 2008:1625
39. Ibid: 1629
40. Essex, 2008:1627
41. Ibid

governments to implement neoliberal economic policies and to develop the political institutions to support these. According to that logic, this will reduce poverty in these countries and reduce the perceived security risk to the US. Of course, this type of instrumental use of aid undermines the sovereignty and democratic accountability of recipient countries.[42] The neoliberal economic agenda is, therefore, the cause of, rather than the solution to poverty, in the Global South.

Within the US, USAID has increasingly come to be seen as overly bureaucratic. The emerging model of the Millennium Challenge Account (MCA) has been contrasted with this, as being less so. It is widely perceived that powerful interests in the US are keen for it to replace USAID as the principle provider of US ODA, and it has the support of powerful neo-Conservative lobby groups.[43]

The Millennium Challenge Account (MCA)
Since 2005, the MCA has existed alongside other US bilateral agencies as a distributor of ODA. It is under the chairpersonship of the Secretary of State (Minister for Foreign Affairs). It functions on the basis of selectivity, focusing its provision of ODA on select countries that conform to a neoliberal policy. In order to qualify for assistance through this fund, recipient governments must demonstrate that they fulfil 16 objectively defined eligibility criteria. These criteria are considered to be indicators of 'ruling justly, investing in their people, and encouraging economic freedom', according to former President George Bush Jnr.[44] This innovation in funding marks a break with the previous system of conditionality, in which countries were required to adopt policy changes in tandem with receiving aid. It places the responsibility on poor countries to comply fully with the required policy changes prior to receiving any funding at all. It is widely believed that the MCA, rather than USAID, represents the future for US bilateral aid.

USAID proved to be a difficult organisation for developing countries to deal with as it has insisted on influencing political

---

42. See chapter 6
43. Chhotray and Hulme, 2009:39
44. Chottray and Hulme, 2009:39

and economic development in those countries. However, the MCA is much more regimented and inflexible. The position on aid is therefore likely to become even more complex. For all kinds of reasons – political, social, historical, cultural or religious, to list a few – not all governments find that they can agree with the pre-conditions being imposed on them by the US through bilateral aid. If the country cannot source US bilateral aid then it must turn to the multilateral agencies. These too, as we have already seen, are mainly controlled by the US, and the aid they provide is subject to US pre-conditions. Using aid as a political weapon inevitably leads to resentment of, and resistance to, US 'interference'. The US is the biggest donor, but that doesn't mean that countries will always look to them for aid. In the same way that an individual doesn't have to go to the biggest name on the high street for a credit card – they can shop around for a credit card company that will offer them the terms and conditions most suited to their needs. The US holds a lot of power at the moment. China, however, is rapidly closing the gap. The US might not be able to continue with uncompromising and unreasonable pre-conditions to aid.

Susan Soederberg[45] has argued that 'while the MCA represents a new departure in terms of a more intrusive, coercive and overtly American-led form of development, its content resembles that of preceding official development agendas'. She sees it as an effort to reward states that adopt pro-market policies – policies which ultimately promote US commercial interests. She contrasts this with the perceived threat to US security represented by 'failed states', and the US government's insistence that governments in these countries gain control of the population through the rule of law, adopt market-led policies and engage with economic globalisation.[46] Chattroy and Hulme[47] broadly concur with Soederberg, in arguing that national security has been at the heart of US foreign assistance since the September 11 attacks in 2001. Chapter 5 of this book discusses the historical motivations behind US ODA in more detail. It highlights in particular the key role of the Cold War in

---

45. 2004:297
46. Ibid: 291-292
47. 2009

determining US aid policy. It should come as no surprise that the new global war that the US is engaged in, the 'War on Terror', should have informed so much of US overseas aid policy in recent years.

A Smaller Donor: United Kingdom (UK) Bilateral Aid

The UK differs in some important respects to the US as a bilateral donor. It has just one coordinating agency for bilateral aid, the Department for International Development (DFID). DFID is an independent department within the UK government. While USAID is under the control of the State Department, DFID is not under the control of the Foreign and Commonwealth Office (FCO). This has enabled DFID, since its inception with the advent of New Labour in 1997, to retain some independence from UK foreign policy and commercial priorities.[48] There have been conflicts between DFID and the FCO, when the promotion of commercial interests by the FCO has come into conflict with DFID's development priorities.[49] Partly due to the independence that DFID has gained in the UK government, it has been able to formally break the links between all ODA from Britain to the purchase of goods or services from UK companies.[50]

Another significant difference between the UK and US approach is that DFID and the UK government do not, formally at least, promote economic policy conditions to aid disbursements – forcing countries to liberalise their economies in order to receive aid. A UK government policy paper states that the UK will only intervene to reduce or stop flows of aid for one of the three following reasons:

a) countries move significantly away from agreed poverty reduction objectives or outcomes or the agreed objectives of a particular aid commitment (e.g. through an unjustifiable rise in military spending, or a substantial deviation from the agreed poverty reduction programme); or

b) countries are in significant violation of human rights or other international obligations; or

c) there is a significant breakdown in partner government

48. Porteous, 2005:281-284
49. Ibid:286.
50. Ibid:282.

financial management and accountability, leading to the risk
of funds being misused through weak administration or corruption.[51]

However, the policy paper goes on to state that the UK will be
guided by IMF assessment of the macroeconomic environment in
recipient countries, and that aid will (in most cases) be conditional
on a favourable IMF assessment of the situation. Since the IMF
only provides favourable assessments to states that implement
neoliberal economic policies, this should be interpreted as a strong
statement of continued economic policy related aid conditionality.
Yet again, even if somewhat indirectly through its influence on
IMF, the US manages to control aid policy.

The DFID approach also differs from the US approach in that
DFID was at the forefront of the move toward direct budget
support for recipient countries. This move was based partly on the
emphasis on a need for 'partnership' with recipient governments
in efforts to tackle poverty. The partnership agenda itself emerged
as part of the new era of aid optimism in the 1990s. The move was
also based around the new belief that states should be supported
to develop institutions of 'good governance' which, in turn,
would promote development objectives. However,[52] direct budget
support has more often than not undermined the institutions of
democratic governance in recipient states.[53] The new enthusiasm
for the state in underdeveloped countries emerged following a
partial acknowledgement of the failures of Structural
Adjustment Policies, but it can really be seen as an effort to
promote the conditions for the protection of the wealth of international commercial interests in those countries.

Furthermore DFID emphasises that it does not seek to intervene
in the policy-making priorities of recipient governments. It claims
to promote the autonomy of these states to determine their own
priorities as 'partners'. The UK government, however, often does
the opposite. For example the UK government has, to a very large

---

51. UK Government, 2005
52. Discussion next chapter
53.

extent, promoted the privatisation of electricity supply in under-developed countries through Globeleq, a DFID owned company.

Globaleq is fully owned by CDC, the British Development Bank, which in turn is fully owned by DFID. In 2006 it had operations in 16 countries across Asia, Latin America and Africa. It is an inter-national power company that focuses solely on 'emerging markets' in underdeveloped countries.[54] Its aim is to promote the privatis-ation of electricity provision in 'developing' countries. Therefore, it has been paying huge sums to multinational corporations that wish to exit from these markets, and taking over their operations. Two US power companies alone received over $1 billion in UK ODA from Globeleq, when they ceased their operations in poor countries.[55]

Joe Zacune, writing for *War on Want*, describes CDC's mission as being to 'pioneer the involvement of the private sector in situ-ations where other companies fear to tread'.[56] Of course privatis-ation of electricity supply often results in poor people being excluded from access to electricity, due to the need to maximise profits and hence keep prices high. Chapter 6 will return to this topic. A senior Bangladesh government official was quoted as saying, 'There is no prospect for unionisation in Globeleq-owned power plants', which reflects the firm's poor record on providing decent employment.[57] While the UK government policy paper states that the UK will not promote particular economic policies in aid recipient countries, the Globaleq example, financed through UK Aid Budget, provides evidence to the contrary.

Promotion of the private sector, through Development Banks, with ODA finance, is not solely a UK phenomenon. It occurs throughout Europe.

Official Equity Investments (OEIs):
The Case of the European Development Banks (DBs)
A set of fourteen national development finance institutions, or

---

54. Zacune, 2006
55. Ibid
56. Ibid:11
57. Ibid:6

DBs, are clustered together in the European Development
Finance Institutions (EDFI) grouping, which is headquartered in
Brussels. These institutions are majority state owned, 'and are
mandated to provide loan finance to private investors and to
invest in private sector enterprises ... under strict market discipline
... [to] non-mature economies'.[58] As outlined earlier, financial
flows of this sort are counted as ODA since they take the form of
OEIs. Storey and Williams (2006) have published a critique of
these organisations, which discusses the role that they play as
development actors. They highlight[59] that half of the EDFI actors
include the promotion of their own domestic firms' operations
overseas as part of their remit. They suggest that although this
does not rule out a potentially positive development outcome for
their activities, these banks are not solely guided by development
concerns. For example, the Danish DB provided finance to Danish
brewer Carlsberg, in tandem with Tibetan partner Tibet Galaxy,
to found a brewery in Tibet to take advantage of a growing market
for beer in the country.[60] Since Tibet is the subject of military occup-
ation by China, such an investment is of grave concern to many
development agencies that are promoting Tibetan independence.
The same bank took part in a joint venture with a Danish company
to produce and supply substitute breast milk (infant formula) to
the Chinese market.[61] Such an investment is of grave concern to
many development agencies that seek to promote public health.
These two examples, provided by the authors, show that the
mandate that DBs often have to promote domestic commercial
interests, and can run counter to promoting positive change in
underdeveloped countries.

These banks may provide credit, at preferential rates, to activities
that the private sector may have supported in any case, resulting in a
problem of 'windfall waste'.[62] An alternative scenario is that
banks finance non-viable projects that the commercial banks will

---

58. EDFI website, in Storey and Williams, 2006:2
59. 2006:11
60. Ibid:9
61. Ibid
62. 2006:12

not touch. Consequently, they have a high proportion of bad debts. As Storey and Williams relate, this can result in Development Banks helping to create an impression in a poor country that, 'SMEs (Small and Medium Enterprises) do not repay their debts', which is damaging to the economy.[63] Of course, other writings view the operation of these DBs as a means of promoting capitalist profit expansion. Such expansion may not be compatible with reducing poverty, and may seek commercial returns for interests in the Global North at the expense of poor people in the Global South.[64]

The Paris Declaration on Aid Effectiveness (PDAE) and the Accra Action Agenda (AAA)

The PDAE was adopted by the DAC in 2005, and formed the basis of the AAA, between aid donors and aid recipients, in 2008. The PDAE laid down a practical road map, agreed by donors, to restructure the global system of ODA. Aid efficiency was high on the agenda. The focus on efficiency was a very welcome development to all who were concerned that ODA was not delivering to its full potential. The PDAE included 56 commitments structured around five core principles: ownership, alignment, harmonisation, managing for results and mutual accountability.

It could reasonably be assumed that if donors and recipient governments adhered to these principles, the effectiveness of aid could be improved. The key principles of PDAE certainly have potential to deliver a major positive impact on effectiveness. Aid is often delivered in a fragmented way by donors. The number of donors and channels through which ODA is delivered, including bilateral aid programmes and NGOs, has increased continuously since the mid-1970s.[65] The example of Vietnam typifies the problem. In 2002, there were approximately 8000 discrete, donor funded projects operating in the country, one for every 9000 people.[66] Generally, each project has its own objectives and reporting require-

---

63. Ibid
64. Ibid
65. Acharya *et al*, 2006:2
66. Ibid

ments. This places a massive burden on the state bureaucracy to try and satisfy the various donor requirements. Such diverse and burdensome administration often distracts recipient governments from setting comprehensive national development objectives.[67] In addition, there are very high and unnecessary transaction costs in the large degree of duplication of effort that this entails. Harmonisation and alignment of donor aid flows could only have the effect of reducing this burden and increasing effectiveness.

Recipient countries ought to have genuine ownership of their development strategies. Increased or strengthened ownership, as a principle of aid delivery, should, therefore, be welcomed as a positive development. However, in welcoming this development, it is important to recognise the challenges that remain in achieving this, especially if donors continue to 'hold the purse strings'. Hyden[68] has shown that in Tanzania, donors have attempted to strengthen government ownership of development policy through the provision of direct budget support. This has certainly strengthened the hand of the Tanzanian government. It has, however, weakened the potential influence of civil society *vis-à-vis* the central government, since the government controls these funds. While this represents a genuine effort on the part of donors to increase the recipient government ownership of development policy, it clearly demonstrates that the practical outworking of this principle is challenging.[69]

The new focus on Aid Effectiveness should be welcomed by all who are concerned to radically alter the dehumanising suffering of underdevelopment. Certainly the language used at the PDAE indicates a willingness to transfer control of the process to developing countries. It would be naïve, however, to conclude that the issue is now fully addressed.

Yash Tandon has commented that:

> On the face of it the Paris Declaration looked benign. It recognised the faults of the existing system, set out reasonably sensible

67. Ibid
68. 2008:268-270
69. Ibid

principles on aid and, significantly, recognised the principle of ownership by the recipient countries, and of mutual accountability between donors and recipients.[70]

The Accra meeting in 2008, at which the AAA was agreed, was the largest ever gathering of the aid industry, with 1200 delegates from around 100 countries in attendance. Despite its size, there are serious concerns that the AAA failed to promote the interests of countries from the Global South.[71] Instead, AAA has been criticised for establishing more mechanisms to further the interests of the donors from the Global North.[72] The links between aid, trade, debt and the creation and perpetuation of poverty did not feature on the Accra agenda. Since, as this book evidences, these links represent the fundamental problem with the global system of ODA, the AAA has, in a very real sense, failed to serve the interests of developing nations. AAA has been criticised for much discussion about achieving the MDGs and addressing poverty, without investigating the causes of poverty.[73] It has been suggested that it's not unusual for donors to frame discussion around development in such a way that the role of global finance in poverty generation is ignored.[74] It's a bit like an arsonist standing in a burning building with a can of petrol in one hand and a box of matches in the other hand, bemoaning the intensity of the heat, and at the same time imposing a set of conditions that must be met before the fire-fighters are allowed in to tackle the blaze.

The AAA failed to create a relationship of mutual accountability between aid donors and aid recipients when it came to performance conditionalities attached to aid. Under the AAA, these would be set

70. Tandon, 2008:108

71. Ibid

72.

73. Ibid

74. For example, one writer has analysed the language used in DFID promotional literature and found that, 'there is never any ... reasons given for the existence of poverty ... there lurks ... an anxiety around the possibility of a rhetorical slippage that could potentially equate the generation of wealth with the creation of poverty ... Such a conflation is only conspicuously avoided in ... careful language.' (Biccum, 2005: 1014)

by the donors and the World Bank and if aid recipients failed to meet the benchmarks for change set for them, aid could be withdrawn.[75] Specifically, the agreement forced recipient countries to seek approval of their budgetary strategies from the World Bank and made provision for the withdrawal of aid if recipient countries did not meet the performance requirements set for them by donors. The implications of this for Southern countries were ignored.[76]

Perhaps the greatest challenge of the AAA is that though it was heralded as promoting predictability of aid flows into the future, there were no binding commitments placed on donors to ensure that predictability.[77] Tandon points out that the AAA did not rule out the use of tied aid into the future, and allowed donors to continue to tie aid to the purchase of goods or services from companies based in the donor country.

Finally, the AAA introduced the principle that 'existing channels' would be used to face 'new global challenges'. This section of the agreement promotes the World Bank as the agency that should finance Southern countries as they address the challenges of climate change. There is, however, significant evidence that the World Bank policies have, historically, caused damage to countries in the South through the conditions it has attached to aid. There is a legitimate fear that the World Bank might gain a new lease of life through this new, potentially vast, stream of funding, and continue to apply these same conditions. The draft agreement assembled by Northern states at the Copenhagen Climate Change Conference at the end of 2009 provides just this opportunity to the World Bank.[78]

Conclusion

In practical outworking, aid, its donors, institutions, and the agreements they have created and manage, is far from benevolent. The policies and actions are a world apart from the sentiment of 'concern to end global poverty' that many believed would follow

75. Ibid:111
76. Ibid
77. Ibid:112
78. Vidal, 2009

the G8 Gleneagles summit in 2005. When examined, the picture that emerges is one in which donor states and the multilateral agencies which they control use aid instrumentally: effecting changes in Southern countries' economic policies that are in the interests of rich economies, promoting commercial interests based in the donor countries and promoting the geopolitical interests of donor states. This creates an environment in which the rich and powerful strengthen their position while the poor become poorer and more marginalised.

The links between aid, trade, debt and the creation and perpetuation of poverty are at the heart of the problem. Until these issues are engaged with wholeheartedly, poverty and marginalisation will continue to increase and recipient countries will continue to suffer. A change of language, without a fundamental change in the *modus operandi* effectively means business as usual. Albert Einstein is reputed to have defined insanity as doing the same thing over and over again and expecting different results.

CHAPTER 4

The Recipients

Large inward financial flows have an impact on the political system and its stability in underdeveloped countries. Where aid flows are volatile, or unpredictable, there are obvious implications for national budgets and the planning of government services. Political elites can use aid to bolster their positions. This undermines accountability to the population at large and consequently undermines democratic governance and state institutions. Given these negative effects, why do poor states continue to accept and seek aid? The answer is partly to do with the system of clientalism that it creates, and partly with the extent to which aid breeds dependency on more aid. Once a country accepts aid, it can very quickly become addicted to it. Instead of breaking that addiction, developed nations and the aid institutions they control often try to strengthen dependency.

Aid Volatility

Aid volatility refers to the varying rates of ODA that recipients receive over time. It also applies to the differences between ODA that is pledged and ODA that is actually paid in a given year. Aid is notoriously volatile and unreliable as a source of state finance. Studies[1] have shown that in countries receiving IMF support, aid flows are much more volatile than domestic revenue collection. The more dependant a country is on ODA (measured by the ratio of ODA to total government revenue), the more volatile are the aid flows that it receives. They also showed that in countries where the IMF interrupted their support, aid flows were up to 80% below commitments.[2] A later study[3] found that in the period

1. Such as Bulir and Hamann (2001) and Bulir and Lane (2002), (reported in Ndaruhutse and Brannelly, 2006:12
2. Ibid
3. Bulir and Hamann, 2005, again reported in Ndaruhutse and Brannelly, 2006

1999-2001, donors promised 50% more aid than they disbursed, and that aid volatility had increased throughout the 1990s. The more recently introduced Poverty Reduction Strategy Programmes (PRSPs) and the Heavily Indebted Poor Country Initiative (HIPC) had not improved aid reliability.[4]

Setting public spending is a notoriously difficult task to perform successfully, for even the most developed nations. The annual spending plan can be subject to many modifications based on dozens of different factors. A sudden, unexpected economic downturn is the most prominent of these. War or a prolonged security response to terrorist activity can also bring about sudden changes in budgetary plans. This annual plan normally falls within a longer term plan, quite often a five year plan, which in itself is subject to change. Imagine how much more difficult making and adhering to these plans would be if the country suddenly found that millions, if not billions of dollars were no longer available. That is the situation in which many developing nations find themselves when aid is suddenly cut off. Governments of poor nations often have to deal with the additional pressures of food shortages and ineffective or nonexistent infrastructures. The challenges for a government in such situations are enormous.

A World Bank study found that aid made up 53.8% of government expenditure in the 50 most aid-dependent countries in the period 1975-1995.[5] In the period 1990-1995, aid to sub-Saharan Africa averaged 50% of public expenditure and 71% of gross investment. In South Asia the figures were 20% and 31% respectively.[6] A World Bank study found that aid to Rwanda was provided on an annual or biannual basis, and that this undermined long term budgetary planning.[7] As Glennie points out, aid volatility is not a good reason to cut aid, but it is a good reason for poor countries to resist becoming too reliant on it.[8] The problem of aid dependence is discussed at the end of this chapter.

---

4. PRSPs are discussed in Chapter 5 and HIPC is discussed in Chapter 8.
5. referred to in Ndaruhutse and Brannelly, 2006:15
6. Foster and Keith, 2004, in Ndaruhutse and Brannelly, 2006:15
7. in Glennie, 2008:70
8. Glennie, 2008:70

Studies have shown that during previous banking crises, ODA has fallen by between 20% and 40%, and has taken years to increase back to pre-crisis levels.[9] This could indicate that a new volatility in aid flows is imminent in the wake of the current global banking crisis. The situation is precarious; ODA fell throughout the 1990s, and only began to pick up again in 2000, with several donors pledging to increase ODA to 0.7 per cent of GNI. The current global economic crisis could undermine these pledges of increased ODA, leading to another devastating period of volatility of aid flows.

Aid and Corruption

It is well known that corruption is an issue in many developing countries. It is also well known that in poor countries that have large amounts of natural resources, a 'resource curse' often exists. This means that the 'windfall' income from oil and mineral wealth does not contribute to improving the lives of the population in general, as it is seized by corrupt political elites. An example of this comes from Africa in 2004. As oil prices boomed, African oil producing countries received a resource 'bonanza', according to Collier.[10] However, he observes that the growth rate of the non-oil part of the economies of these countries was identical to the rest of Africa during that year. Aid can function in the same way, with the poor being excluded from its benefits because it is misappropriated by elites. As Djankov et al[11] record, 'Natural resources and foreign aid share a common characteristic: they can be appropriated by corrupt politicians without having to resort to unpopular, and normally less profitable, measures like taxation.'

Djankov et al[12] describe the means by which aid is corruptly diverted from its intended destination as 'rent seeking' behaviour. Rent seeking refers to people seeking private benefit through the political arena, and occurs especially when large amounts of finance are transferred with little oversight (such as can be the

---

9. UNCTAD, 2009:1
10. 2006
11. Djankov et al, 2008:2
12. Ibid:171

case with ODA). For example, in Uganda, during the period 1991-1995, schools received only 13% of the aid that was provided as ear-marked grants, and received by government.[13] In Somalia, some have argued that the civil war was provoked by the efforts of competing groups to gain control of food aid.[14]

Aid can also fuel corruption, by providing a disincentive to the public to maintain oversight of government income.[15] In a situation where leaders need to rely on the general population to raise taxes, there is an incentive for the public to maintain oversight of the activities of these leaders and the uses to which government income is put. In a situation in which government income does not arise from taxation (such as when oil revenues or ODA makes up a large part of government income), there is less incentive to maintain oversight of how this money is spent.[16] Glennie comments:

> State accountability has grown side by side with taxation. Conversely, when a large proportion of the money needed by the state is available from a source other than its citizens, the development of state accountability is retarded.[17]

Sub-Saharan Africa is a case in point. Overall, sub-Saharan African countries take far less tax revenue than developed countries, making up the difference with ODA receipts. There is evidence that shows that receiving ODA acts as a disincentive to raising taxes in recipient countries.[18]

At the extreme, aid can perpetuate the rule of an autocratic and corrupt ruler.[19] In Zimbabwe in 2001, Robert Mugabe's rule was perpetuated in the midst of extreme food shortages, by the intervention of the UN World Food Programme to feed millions of people. Although it was arguably essential for the UN to intervene, a consequence of this intervention was that Mugabe held

13. Ibid:172
14. Ibid
15. Glennie, 2008:71
16. Collier, 2006:1484
17. 2008:75
18. Ibid
19. Glennie 2008:72

onto power in the elections that year. There is no doubt that such intervention can be complicated and that the arguments from both sides, for and against, are very passionate. From a moral point of view, would it have been right for the UN to let thousands of people starve so that Mugabe was removed from power? On the other side of the argument, was it right to prop up Mugabe's tyrannical regime, and in the process condemn thousands to torture and death? Sometimes the honourable path is not very clear.

African leaders stay in power for an average of twelve years – three times the Western average. This partly as a result of aid.[20] This is often because when government policies fail, a country suffers a downturn, 'or decisions are made to strengthen the army rather than basic services',[21] and the consequences a normal government might experience are dampened because aid steps in.[22] Another study[23] evidenced that, in the long run, continued aid assists autocratic rulers more than democratic ones, because they stockpile aid for use in mitigating future shocks, whilst democratic leaders must spend it.

Accountability, Institutions and Democracy
As evidenced, by substituting for domestic taxation, aid can undermine the accountability of governments downward to the population. This lack of downward accountability is often compounded by donor reporting requirements. Where donors demand accountability the direction of accountability shifts outwards, i.e. to donors, away from the people. This not only undermines accountability to the people but also undermines the institutions of the state.

In a functioning democracy, the electorate is able to hold the government to account at the ballot box. They can elect an alternative government if the incumbent fails to deliver promised policy changes. However, in many poor countries, the electorate knows all too well that the really important decisions are taken by multi-

20. Ibid:73
21. Ibid
22. Ibid
23. Kono and Montinola 2009

lateral institutions such as the IMF and World Bank, or major bilateral donors such as the US, and that the government is really accountable to them. This undermines the trust that the electorate could and should have in their ability to use the electoral system to change the policy direction of the state. This political order provides the government with a convenient excuse when it has to make an unpopular policy decision. Government can simply blame the IMF or World Bank.

The interruption of conditions imposed on a country by organisations such as the IMF can also be used by the governments of poor nations to impose entirely self-serving policies on their citizens. Conditions such as security and civil stability can be used to brutally crack down on any opposition within their country. Other conditions provide a convenient excuse to displace communities within a country in order to access natural resources. When such abuses take place the donor countries often turn a blind eye – as long as the wider strategy of the donor countries remain on track, human rights can simply be ignored.

The primary mechanism by which aid recipient governments are made accountable to external donors is through the conditions attached to ODA. These are requirements, imposed by donors, (whether multilateral or bilateral). These policy requirements or conditions must be fulfilled in order for the recipient government to to receive ODA. Throughout the 1980s and into the 1990s, as Chapters 5 and 6 illustrate, conditions were enforced on recipient countries through Structural Adjustment Policies (SAPs). These policies, imposed by the IMF and World Bank, forced underdeveloped countries to adopt a range of policies to promote market provision of services, the free operation of market forces, and massive cuts in public spending. The outcomes of these policies are discussed in later chapters. For the moment it is enough to understand that these conditions actively undermined the democratic process in the poor countries that were subjected to them, since the government became accountable to outside donors rather than to the population.

An example of how donor conditionality has undermined both the democratic process and institutional accountability can be found in Tanzania's recent experience. The country has often been held up as an example of how donors can work well with aid recipients.[24] However, a recent study found that it was difficult to discern any significant divergence between the policy priorities of the governing party and those of the majority of donors. It was observed that the likelihood is that, 'the Tanzanian government is not leading but following and is developing policies which respond to what it knows to be donor preferences'.[25] Meanwhile, Ghana's budgetary process, 'has been described as a "façade" and a deceptive "mirage",'[26] because of the extent to which it is designed to simply appeal to donors' priorities. Glennie goes so far as to suggest that in sub-Saharan Africa, 'the problem of self-censorship now pervades African government policymaking'.[27] In short, these governments need the aid and they have become experts at saying and doing all the right things in order to get that aid, regardless of the consequences for their own population.

More recently, these conditions have been joined by others which encourage underdeveloped countries to improve the institutions that are needed to allow free market economics to operate effectively. These include requirements for poor countries to establish functioning legal systems that can protect and promote property rights, functioning anti-corruption systems, predictable and functioning taxation systems, and other state institutions. Much of this reform is intended to improve the capacity of the state to function, and for the state to operate along the lines of procedural democracy. Ironically, however, the very fact that these conditions are forced on poor countries often subverts the democratic process. It could be argued that this also contributes to undermining the accountability of the institutions of government to the people. It is significant that 50% of World Bank loan conditions now relate to governance criteria, compared to just 17% at the end of the 1990s.[28]

The Kenyan constitutional crisis in 2000 demonstrates how

24. Glennie, 2008:60
25. Ibid:61
26. Ibid
27. Ibid:62
28. Glennie, 2008:58

conditionality can undermine the institution of government. In that year, the IMF withheld aid when the country's High Court ruled that the recently created Anti-Corruption Authority was unconstitutional.[29] It has been suggested that this may have been the right thing to do at the time, given the importance of functioning anti-corruption institutions for African societies.[30] Kenya's Attorney General drafted a bill which he showed to the IMF before showing to the parliament. This affair drastically undermined Kenya's struggling democracy, since it implied that its court system could be overruled by the IMF and that the legislative process in the country was a matter in which the parliament appeared not to be in control. According to liberal democratic theory, the people are only sovereign if their government is answerable to them alone, in making decisions. There is a strange paradox when democratic governance and the institutions of governance can be undermined by donor conditions which purport to enhance these institutions.

It is right for donor countries to try to enhance the rights of individuals within a country, but it is not right to go over the heads of the voting public in that country when doing this. No developed country would accept that level of outside pressure. There would be massive outcry if the government of a developed nation had to take new laws to an outside nation for approval. The resentment that this instils in a nation could last for generations.

Clientalism and Aid Dependency

The question introduced at the start of this chapter, was why, given these negative effects of aid, do recipient countries continue to seek further contributions of ODA? The answer to this question lies partly with clientalism, and partly with aid dependency, which aid itself fosters. Clientalism is a system based on patron/client relationships. As long as those in power have control of the resources that ODA provides, and there is little oversight of how these funds are dispersed, political elites can maintain support by gifting those who are loyal to them with these resources. This rela-

---

29. Glennie, 2008:58
30. Ibid

tionship is a classic example of that of the patron and the client. In this situation, ODA may not be put to work to promote development in the country in question, but it does function to enable those in power to remain in power, and to command loyalty. ODA has been shown to have maintained autocratic leaders in positions of power and to have perpetuated the rule of leaders in sub-Saharan Africa. From the donor's point of view, giving ODA provides them with a large degree of leverage over policy formation in poor countries, and enables them to maintain compliant leaders in power in the recipient country. As long as the leaders of a developing nation are complying with the broad terms set out by the donor nations, then the donor nations can be less concerned with the situation on the ground in that country. In these circumstances, individual poverty is not seen as important – yet that is the very thing that aid is supposed to be addressing.

In his review of literature in the area, Kilby[31] has reported the observation that some countries tend to vote in line with US concerns at the UN, even when it is against their interests to do so and when, in different circumstances, they would not. These countries, interestingly enough, tend to receive more IMF loans than countries that do not. It's obvious, therefore, that loyalty (in this case measured by voting patterns at the UN) is rewarded in terms of ODA. In addition, compliance with conditionalities can be seen as a direct means of displaying support for donor priorities. This is an objective requirement for countries in order for them to receive aid disbursements. In these ways, donors enter into clientalist relationships with recipient governments just as much as the governments in recipient countries enter into clientalist relationships with those whose support they need to remain in power. All of this contributes to the maintenance of the *status quo* of the international system of ODA, rather than to a questioning of its effectiveness, by both donor and recipient governments.

An obvious reason for poor countries to continue seeking ODA is that they do not have an alternative means of financing the operation of the state. In many poor countries ODA makes up

31. 2009:52

a large proportion of government spending. In many cases ODA is one of the largest sectors of recipient countries' economies. Some specific examples further highlight this point: in Burkina Faso, in the period 1985-1989, aid made up two-thirds of the national budget and 8% of GDP.[32] In the period 1990-1999, Zambia, Malawi, Mozambique, Guinea-Bissau and Burundi all received more than 25% of total GNP in ODA, with Guinea-Bissau receiving nearly half of its GNP in the form of ODA.[33]

More recently, aid to Africa has doubled, and donors have pledged that further increases in aid to the region will be made. This can only imply that these countries are even more dependent on ODA now than these statistics suggest. On that basis, the future holds a grim prospect of even greater aid dependence. As we have seen, ODA provides a disincentive to governments to raise tax revenue. Therefore, the more ODA that these countries receive, the less possible it becomes for them to escape from reliance on aid, through raising domestic revenue. In this sense aid dependence becomes a vicious cycle. Aid dependence has emerged as part of a wider process in which the countries of the Global North have encouraged the countries of the Global South to become economically dependent upon them. Dependency facilitates the extraction of resources and wealth. Structures of dependence between the donor countries and the recipient countries have emerged. Tandon states:

These structures are reinforced by aid, among other tools of Northern control, including the Bretton Woods institutions, and the ideology of market fundamentalism, including its current incarnation, neoliberal globalisation.[34]

Chapter 5 outlines the role that aid played, from the post-colonial era to the present, in structuring the exploitation of the Global South by the Global North. Chapter 6 outlines the role that aid has played in furthering liberalisation of global economics and considers the effects of this on poor people in underdeveloped countries. It highlights the degree to which aid functions to

---

32. Djankov *et al*, 2008:170
33. Sogge, 2002:222
34. 2008:76

support this wider strategy and aims to fully control the economies and people of the Global South.

When the media consider volumes of ODA that are transferred, the emphasis is typically on the percentage of donor GNI that is transferred as ODA. There is little consideration of the amount of recipient country GNI that is received as ODA. This is absurd, since levels of ODA must surely be best assessed most accurately from a demand, rather than a supply side.[35] Analysing volumes of aid by the current convention has the convenient result of deflecting attention from the reality of aid dependence.

Aid dependence is more than simply a matter of financial arithmetic which can easily be measured by assessing the ratio of aid to GNP or the reliance of the government's budget on aid money. Dependence on aid has a psychological dimension. Yet again, Yash Tandon's comments on aid dependence are insightful.

> A psychology of aid dependence among the peoples of the South, reinforced by a lack of self confidence in their own ability ... and a lack of courage to displease donors by failing to show gratitude for their generosity. Disillusioned with the policies and corruption of their leaders, the ordinary people are sometimes even more inclined to seek out assistance to get them out of their current predicament.[36]

Glennie[37] describes this psychology as a 'sense of powerlessness that has been instilled in governments, the civil service, parliaments and civil society in nearly all [sub-Saharan] African countries'. He is commenting on Africa, but aid dependence is obviously common to other regions also. He describes the condition as being characterised by, 'a lack of initiative in developing strategies and policies and, in general, a reactive rather than proactive form of government'.[38]

The point here is not to suggest that African or any other people possess some kind of psychological deficiency. It is rather to

---

35. Glennie, 2008:24
36. Tandon 2008:76
37. 2008:55
38. Ibid

assert that this psychological condition is a rational response to working under a system in which donors set the agenda through aid conditionalities. In such circumstances national governments, civil society groups etc, have very little say in the policies that are pursued. There is little incentive to display initiative if you do not have enough power to carry out your plans. Furthermore, it is rational for ordinary people to look to donors for solutions to their problems when domestic elites and governments fail to offer any.

Many poor countries are becoming more and more dependent on aid as time passes, rather than less so. Although promises of ODA into the future continue to be made, it is not guaranteed to last forever. Poor countries will eventually have to find some means of developing in the absence of aid. Unfortunately, the emergence of these alternatives is hampered by the dependency that aid breeds. If aid is cut off, a poverty catastrophe awaits in countries that experienced years of corruption, a lack of investment in infrastructure or industries capable of supporting self-sufficiency. Such a catastrophe is likely to be more devastating than anything that has gone before.

Conclusion
ODA has many damaging effects on the political system in poor countries. The volatility of aid flows undermines the ability of poor countries to plan their budgets on a multiannual basis. In situations where countries are heavily aid dependent, volatility of aid flows can undermine the state's ability to pay for essential social services.

Aid also undermines the accountability of the government to the people in aid recipient countries. It replaces this accountability with accountability outward, from the government to donors. When this happens, governments in recipient countries lose the ability to implement policy autonomously, and democratic institutions are undermined.

The aid system is often perpetuated, not by a genuine concern to encourage development, but by a clientalist system of patronage. Within this system, those with power, including donors,

recipient governments, and the political power brokers in recipient countries, all obtain benefits from the aid system. As a result
they have an interest in perpetuating its existence. Paradoxically
aid dependence is a further crucial reason why poor countries
continue to seek ODA flows from donors. Flows of aid bring
about a reliance on future flows of aid, creating a vicious cycle of
aid dependence, as sources of domestic revenue dry up.

CHAPTER 5

A History of Aid

The nature of Official Development Assistance (ODA) has changed over the period from its inception at the end of the second World War. The evolution of that development includes an era of state-led 'Import Substitution Industrialisation' development in the 1950s and 60s, a period of integrated rural development of the 1970s, the Structural Adjustment policies of the 1980s and 1990s and the recent development of a 'new aid architecture' from 2000. It is useful, in understanding the context to aid in the post World War II world, to have a brief overview of how global poverty and inequality have been created and reinforced through the relationship of colonial powers to their colonies.

Aid has facilitated the emergence of a new form of imperialism, which has replaced the era of colonial imperialism. According to Duménil and Lévy,[1] imperialism does not refer to a particular phase in capitalist development, but has been one of its defining features. They define imperialism as 'the economic advantage taken by the most advanced and dominating countries over less developed or vulnerable regions of the world'.[2] They suggest that this process does not have to take the form of direct domination by force, although this was the case in the colonial era and is often the case today. Imperialism can be facilitated by putting in place governments that are 'prone to the development of economic relations favourable to the interests of dominating countries'.[3] Aid has played this role since the emergence of the Bretton Woods system of global economic governance at the end of the Second World War (WWII). It is a more subtle form of oppression and control than that witnessed at the height of the old colonial empires.

1. 2004
2. 2004:660
3. Ibid

Nevertheless, the legacy of economic dependency that is being established through aid today will endure for decades to come – lasting as long as, if not longer than even colonial imperialism did. Through aid, the US is seen by many to be spearheading this new imperial march, a fact that has not been lost on radical terrorist groups as they search for new safe havens and new recruits. In this sense, the use of aid as an imperial tool is incredibly dangerous in terms of international stability. History has taught us that poor nations cannot be eternally exploited. Eventually pressure builds and revolution comes. History has also shown us that resolution of inequality often comes through conflict. The seeds of resentment being sown today in many of the world's poorest nations will someday bear fruit that will be catastrophic to our world. At the end of WWII the US was the only superpower intact. It was US loans which rebuilt Britain, France, Germany and other countries that had been devastated through the conflict. It is an interesting side note that the US made progressive dissolution of European colonies a pre-requisite for this assistance. At that time it may have been viewed as a very moral stance for the US to take, but today the US has replaced the old world imperialists as masters of those countries that they once fought so hard to free.

The global system of Official Development Assistance (ODA) was established as the ashes of WWII cooled. The chaos and destruction of the war provided a clean slate on which to develop a new geo-political logic. This logic was determined by the emerging Cold War on the one hand, and the process of European decolonisation on the other.

Prior to the war, colonial domination of subject peoples had enabled European development. It enabled industrialisation in Europe and inflicted terrible poverty and underdevelopment on whole populations in the colonies. The world that emerged out of WWII was divided into the industrialised West, the Soviet, nominally communist, East and a majority Third World, consisting of the post-colonial, newly independent states.[4] The West and East battled for control of and support from Third World states.

4. McMichael, 2008:chap 2

The strategic use of ODA became a crucial factor in US efforts to win support for the West.

The colonial period
India's colonial experience is a useful example to outline the role that colonialism played in restructuring the world economy, undermining the economies of colonised regions. Bengal was considered one of the wealthiest regions in the world by British colonists who arrived there in the eighteenth century, with Dacca (the capital of modern day Bangladesh) in particular, considered to be a city richer than London. The region had a sophisticated weaving industry which the colonists sought to exploit. The British East India Company gained control of Bengal in the eighteenth century and set about extracting cloth at a fraction of its value from the weavers. This was done through 'fines, imprisonments, floggings, forcing bonds from them, etc', as an English merchant wrote in 1772. This practice of super-exploitation[5] led to the impoverishment of Bengal.[6]

The cheap cultivation of cotton by slave labour and the development of steam engine spinning factories in England led to the ultimate collapse of the weaving industry throughout India. India was opened up for cheap imports of textiles from Britain in 1813. The de-industrialisation effect was estimated to be equivalent to 55-75% of national consumption in the period 1870-1880.[7] The weaving industry in India was actively dismantled by Britain. As a result, the Indian cotton production would no longer support an industry that generated wealth for India. Instead it supported the development of the emergent British textiles industry. This was a major source of wealth generation for British industrialists, enabling them to consolidate their positions and control through capital accumulation. It also led to industrialisation in Britain's northern cities. This was the manner in which the development of the United Kingdom was facilitated by the creation of *under*-development in her colony.

---

5. This term is explained later in this section
6. Lines, 2008:30-33
7. Lines, 2008:30-33

Similar processes were repeated throughout the European colonies. The dominant relationship was characterised by gaining control of primary products from colonial satellites for manufacturing in European centres (or metro-poles). Often they were resold in colonies as manufactured imports (termed the colonial division of labour).[8] This division of labour enabled the generation of large profits which accrued to wealthy investors and elites in the European metro-poles. Meanwhile, the control of food-stuffs from the colonies provided food security to the growing industrial work force in European cities. This process effectively remodelled colonial economies, as they became dependent, as exporters of primary products (or commodities), on their relationship with their colonial power. Many Third World countries' economies continue, to this day, to be dependent on exporting a narrow range of commodities to industrialised Northern countries. This situation which was created in the colonial era continues to be perpetuated by imperialism, and facilitated by ODA.

Many colonies became plantation economies, based around large-scale mono-cropping, on plantations run by European farmers. These plantations required taking control of land from the indigenous people. Indigenous peoples where progressively forced onto smaller and smaller landholdings. On these holdings they had to provide the means of subsistence for a growing population, many of whom were seasonal labourers on the plantations. By this process, the local populations absorbed the cost of providing labour to the benefit of the colonial plantation owners. Since the household provided the means of subsistence (although barely), wages could be set at less than that required to provide subsistence (a situation known as 'super-exploitation'). This process was repeated in South East Asia, Africa and in the Latin American '*latifundo-minifundo*' relationship. It was a process that not only greatly benefited the colonial elite, but created widespread poverty amongst rural populations in the colonies.[9] European development was achieved on the backs of peasant farmers in the colonies, through the colonial division of labour.

8. McMichael, 2008:31
9. Bello 2009: chap 1

In Africa, the continent was divided into dozens of protect-orates and colonies during the European 'scramble for Africa' in the nineteenth century. Each was administered separately, unlike India which was centrally administered by the British. Africa was directly colonised for a much shorter period of time than many other colonised regions, which partly explains why it never developed markets for manufactured imports.[10] After slavery in the early nineteenth century, Africa was ruled by foreign powers who transformed her economies to 'facilitate the extraction of wealth wherever possible'.[11] By exporting primary commodities, Africa was restructured more radically than any other region during its relatively brief experience of colonial rule. However, despite being radically restructured to face outward to the world economy, the continent did not develop the internal markets that developed elsewhere.[12] For example, roads were not built to link up different regions within Africa, but went straight to the coast, to facilitate the export of commodities.

Decolonisation
Widespread decolonisation peaked after the end of WWII. The European powers, weakened by the war, could not resist the rise of anti-colonial independence movements. They did, however, seek to maintain the basis of their economic relationship with their former colonies. As the British Committee on Colonial Policy advised the prime minister in 1957,

> During the period when we can still exercise control in any terri-tory, it is most important to take every step open to us to ensure, as far as we can, that British standards and methods of business and administration permeate the whole life of the territory.[13]

The central means by which this control was to be exercised was through the formation of nation-states, along the lines of the nation-states that had arisen in Europe in the nineteenth century.

---

10. Lines, 2008:33-34
11. Ibid
12. Ibid
13. quoted in, McMichael, 2008, 47

The European powers insisted on the nation state as the basis of the post-colonial political formation, since they saw it as 'a vehicle for the containment of political desires and of extraction of resources via European military and *economic aid* [my emphasis], investment, and trade'.[14] Local elites in the colonies saw their interests as bound up with gaining control of these new nation states. As McMichael wrote, 'the power its members assumed was already mortgaged to the nation state system'.[15]

When elites gained control of the state, maintaining a positive relationship with the former colonial power and the newly dominant United States (US) was generally a priority. A relationship that continued to foster control of resources by western powers was usually considered priority. Nevertheless, this was regarded as the necessary price to pay for the power and riches that control of the state entailed. The relationship that became established between former colonial powers and the US, on the one hand, and post-colonial states on the other, was one of patron and client. In some cases, the former colonies lined up with the communist East as the patron. Mobutu in Zaire even played the West and East off each other.

The US emerged from WWII as a superpower. It had followed a path that had internalised the colonial division of labour, through the relationship of exchange between the agricultural Southern and mid-Western states and the industrial Eastern states.[16] This process had allowed the US to develop as an industrialised power, since it was not exporting its wealth in the way the colonies were. The use of African slave labour had greatly contributed to the accumulation of wealth in the country. Alone among major industrial countries, the US had not fought a war on its own soil. Furthermore, the manufacturing boom of the war economy had allowed it to recover from the economic depression of the 1930s. The US faced two major obstacles in the post-war period. The first was the economic ruin of Europe, which had been caused by the war. The US needed Europe as a trading partner.

14. McMichael, 2008:47
15. Ibid
16. McMichael, 2008:42

The other was the rise of Russia as a competing communist super-power. ODA became a crucial tool in the face of both of these obstacles.

The establishment of the International Financial Institutions (IFIs) and the 'Bretton Woods' system

Representatives of 45 countries met in Bretton Woods in the United States in 1944 to devise a post-war economic system that would avert economic shocks such as the Great Depression of the 1930s, widely held to have led to WWII. The International Monetary Fund (IMF) and the World Bank (initially known as the International Bank for Reconstruction and Development (IBRD)) were created at this meeting. The purpose of the IMF was to provide a stable global monetary system that would facilitate global trade and capital accumulation. The IBRD was to provide US finance for the reconstruction of Western Europe, also necessary to facilitate future capital accumulation.[17] The US has always been the major investor in these IFIs. This fact has, historically, enabled it to control their policies and practices. Up until 1947, the majority of IBRD lending was to provide US finance for European reconstruction.

The US was particularly concerned about the rise of communist political parties in Europe at that time. The Truman administration decided that an aid effort much larger than one the IBRD could facilitate was required, so the Marshall Plan was instituted in 1947. Its purpose was to win over the populations of Western Europe to liberal democratic ideals and politics, through a rapid economic boost provided by aid. The Marshall plan entailed direct bilateral (government to government) aid of unprecedented levels to a number of Western European states. This freed up the World Bank to engage in lending to Third World countries for the official purpose of development assistance.[18]

The Cold War rationale for aid to the Third World

The ideological justification that underpinned this new departure of US aid to the Third World was elaborated by President Truman

---

17. Boas and McNeill, 2003:16
18. Boas and McNeill, 2003:53

in his inaugural address in 1949: 'We must embark on a bold new programme for making the benefits of our scientific advances and industrial progress available for the improvement and growth of underdeveloped areas. More than half of the people of the world are living in conditions approaching misery ... Their economic life is primitive and stagnant. Their poverty is a handicap and threat both to them and more prosperous areas. For the first time in history, humanity possesses the knowledge and skills to relieve the suffering of these people ... The old imperialism – exploitation for foreign profit – has no place in our plans – Greater productivity is the key to prosperity and peace. And the key to greater production is wider and more vigorous application of modern scientific and technical knowledge.'[19]

Truman divided the world into those who were 'developed' or 'modern' on the one hand and those who were 'primitive', 'traditional' or 'underdeveloped' on the other. The purpose of ODA, according to the official thinking, was to assist in bridging this gap, in bringing the underdeveloped majority of the world's population to the point of being developed. In other words, to the point of being like the West.

Commenting on Truman's address, the Mexican Intellectual Gustavo Esteva has pointed out that:

> Underdevelopment began, then, on January 20 1949. On that day, two billion people became underdeveloped. In a real sense, from that time on, they ceased being what they are, in all their diversity, and were transmogrified into an inverted mirror of other's reality: a mirror that defines their identity ... simply in the terms of a homogenising and narrow minority.[20]

Not only did these two billion people become underdeveloped at that time, but according to that thinking, the role of the West would be to assist them in 'developing' along a path that would lead their societies to be mirrors of the West. Since then orthodox accounts of development aid generally cast it in the role of performing this benevolent function. Since the relationships

19. quoted in Boas and McNeill, 2003:7
20. quoted in McMichael, 2008:45

fostered through aid, between developed and underdeveloped countries, have been structured around benefiting interests in donor countries, promoting development in the Third World, when it has occurred (such as in South Korea), has only been a concern in so far as it has benefited these interests.

Walt Rostow, an influential economist, formulated his 'modernisation theory' to explain how 'traditional' societies could develop in a linear fashion toward modern societies. Eventually, along that linear progression, they would be a mirror of the rich North.[21] Rostow assumed that this process could be accelerated by the transfer of knowledge, technology and aid from rich to poor countries. His theory chimed with Truman's ideological justification for aid. He was very clear in linking this development agenda to what he saw as the urgent threat to US influence in the world from Soviet communism. He was also clear to link it to the urgent need to protect US access to raw materials in the Third World. He wrote:

> The location, natural resources, and populations of the underdeveloped areas are such that, should they become effectively attached to the Communist bloc, the United States would become the second power in the world ... Indirectly, the evolution of the underdeveloped areas is likely to determine the fate of ... those industrialised regions in the free world alliance we are committed to lead ... In short, our military security and our way of life, as well as the fate of Western Europe and Japan, are at stake in the evolution of the underdeveloped areas.[22]

This logic was shared by the US administration and became the determining factor in US and World Bank aid disbursements in the post WWII period. A major goal of World Bank lending at the time was to secure support for the West in the Cold War. Sometimes this was achieved through aid to support economic development along Western norms. At other times it was achieved by supporting compliant dictators who would remain on the side of the West. Access to the raw materials of these states

---

21. Rostow, 1960
22. quoted in McMichael, 2008:62

could be assured through the economic and political dependency that aid fostered. Another key goal was to ensure markets for the products of industrialised capitalist countries.

The US supported dictators during the Cold War, regardless of their brutality or crimes against humanity. Allegiance with the West against the Soviet East was at stake. This support was often provided in the form of aid. In 1976, the World Bank was encouraged, by the US government, to issue large loans to General Pinochet[23] in Chile despite his appalling human rights record.[24] The only important factor in their consideration was that he had successfully overthrown a popular socialist revolution (with CIA help), and ought therefore to be supported. The US also provided aid to corrupt dictators, even when they embezzled these funds. The CIA brought President Mobutu to power in the Congo (which he renamed Zaire) in 1965. By the late 1970s he had amassed a huge personal fortune through cornering as much as half of US aid to sub-Saharan Africa.[25] As long as he acted as a bulwark against communism in the region, the aid kept flowing.

Aid was often cut when governments adopted left-wing policies such as nationalising industries. When these governments were overthrown by coups, and in many cases replaced by brutal military regimes, the aid was reinstated. Chile, Brazil and Indonesia provided clear examples of this aid being used to undercut rival, socialist, political movements.[26] During the Cold War, aid flowed disproportionately to states that were considered of strategic geographic importance in the battle against communism. Western aid flowed to regionally powerful states such as South Korea, Israel, Turkey and Iran.[27]

These policies may not sound familiar, especially when viewed

---

23. Pinochet, who ruled as a fascist dictator, came to power in Chile in a CIA backed coup, which overthrew a democratically elected, socialist government in the country, which enjoyed widespread support. Chilean democracy never recovered from this experience, and the military still have a strong hold over political decision making in the country.

24. Hayter, 1990:89

25. McMichael, 2008:60

26. Hayter and Watson, 1985:17

27. Ibid:61-62

in the modern context of aid as heralded at Gleneagles. One might be disposed to view them as the unfortunate remnants of a bygone, less enlightened age. We might look back with amusement on the West's fear and paranoia concerning an expanding Soviet empire. But, are we any more politically sophisticated today than people living through that time? The aid given to despots in the name of 'freedom' was ill-conceived. Nowadays we consider ourselves more globally aware. We would never sit back and allow our governments to support such regimes. Would we? One act of terrorism, albeit a sickening and spectacular one, has provided a new generation of Western politicians licence to engage in policies not too dissimilar to those adopted by their Cold War forerunners. The *War on Terror* has been, and will continue to be used to justify channeling from where there is genuine need to where it will buy good will and loyalty for the US. The survival of barely democratic governments, such as the one in Afghanistan, or worse still wholly undemocratic governments, is facilitated by Western support.

Aid for Import Substitution Industrialisation: 1950s and 1960s
Economic nationalism dominated Third World states' economic policies during this period. This philosophy sought to reverse the colonial division of labour by allowing industrial production to develop behind protective barriers, such as tariffs and import controls. This shifted resources away from importing manufactured products and toward domestic manufacturing. The era was known as that of 'Import Substitution Industrialisation', because Third World states attempted to reduce their reliance on imports. They industrialised by manufacturing those products that they previously imported.

Industry, rather than labour intensive agriculture, was seen as the best way for development. The result was a transfer of resources, including labour, food and raw materials, from rural to urban areas. Increases in agricultural productivity were fuelled by the mechanisation of agriculture. This allowed resources to flow from agriculture into the industrial sector. Unfortunately the reality was that industrialisation was pursued at the expense of the rural poor – they were left behind and not swept along with this change.

During its first 20 years of existence, the World Bank supported efforts toward industrialisation with large-scale loans to the Third World. These were issued at preferential interest rates, for national infrastructural projects such as dams, highways and power plants. Two thirds of World Bank loans went to supporting electrification and transportation systems during this period. In reality, multinational corporations (MNCs) 'hopped over' the protectionist walls of Third World states and often bought up most of the major industries, such was the case in Brazil, Peru and Venezuela, where US capitalist interests controlled most large industries by 1956.[28] From the perspective of the US, large scale infrastructural investments were necessary for the profitable operation of US corporations in these countries, and were promoted for this reason.

Bilateral aid also flowed toward these projects. It was generally 'tied', by the donors, to the purchase of manufactured inputs and services from businesses in the donor country. The average price of goods purchased through tied aid conditions has been found to be 25% higher than world market prices. That shouldn't be surprising.[30] Technological development is a progressive process. New technologies follow on from, and rely heavily on the skills associated with previous developments. For example, it you took the most modern car from today and gave it to people living in the UK or US back at the start of the twentieth century, it would be completely useless to them. The fuel available would damage the catalytic convertor and destroy the injector system; the computer controlled components (along with most other components) would have no one available with the skills needed to service them. Some of the technology being sold to developing nations was the best money could buy; state of the art; top of the range, and almost completely useless to them. To make them work required the purchase of a whole range of additional technologies and services, which they were also obligated to source from their donor countries.

28. McMichael, 2008:52
29. Hayter, 1990:84
30. Degnbol-Martinussen and Engberg-Pedersen, 2003:44-45

The World Bank only covered the foreign exchange costs of these projects in its lending. This promoted a dependence on imported technologies. This creation of dependence on imports from donor countries was a deliberate goal of aid in the post war years. It still is.[31] Commenting in the 1950s, then President of the World Bank, Eugene Black stated:

> Our foreign aid programmes constitute a distinct benefit to American business. The three major benefits are: (1) foreign aid provides a substantial and immediate market for United States goods and services. (2) foreign aid stimulates the development of new overseas markets for United States companies. (3) foreign aid orients national economies toward a free enterprise system in which United States firms can prosper.[32]

President Nixon was rather more blunt during his 1968 election campaign: 'Let us remember that the main point of development aid is not to help other nations but to help ourselves.'[33]

By moving funds to regions that needed purchasing power, the World Bank encouraged world economic growth and trade. This primarily benefited western interests.[34]

The Third World was expected to achieve rapid industrialisation facilitated by this system of aid. To an extent this was achieved. The Newly Industrialised Countries (NICS), Hong Kong, Singapore, Taiwan, South Korea, Brazil and Mexico experienced spectacular economic growth during the 1960s. In the case of South Korea, it has been commented that its success 'should be no surprise', since countries like the United States, Japan and West Germany and organisations like the World Bank and the International Monetary Fund have participated in planning South Korean development.[35] The South Korean economic policy ministry had representatives of the World Bank and IMF on its staff.[36] South Korea's development was micro-managed because

---

31. see chapter 6
32. quoted in Hayter, 1990:83
33. Ibid:84
34. McMichael, 2008:chapter 3
35. Cummings, quoted in Hayter, 1990:85
36. Ibid

of geographical and geopolitical significance in the Cold War. The success of these countries also demonstrated the unbalanced nature of development in the Third World. Yet they also provide a very clear indication of just what is possible when there is enough international will to make a difference.

The NIC economies cornered the bulk of foreign private investment. Consequently much of their manufacturing for export came to be controlled by MNCs. In other regions industrialisation failed to occur: In Africa, manufacturing only accounted for 5% of Gross Domestic Product (GDP) by 1975, as the extraction of commodities was prioritised by the capitalist West.[37] In most parts of the Third World there was little consideration for the distribution of the benefits of economic growth. Neither did the World Bank seem interested in this when making assessments regarding loan decisions. A major criticism of this era of aid was that the benefits of economic growth did not succeed in trickling down to the poor, especially those living in rural areas.

Aid and the rural poor: 1950s and 1960s

Industrialisation was pursued at the expense of the rural poor during this period. Providing cheap food to urban workers was prioritised above providing agricultural prices that could enable peasants to subsist. The peasantry in Third World countries found themselves increasingly exploited by landlords who, as a result of the commercialisation of agriculture, sought to reduce their labour costs. This was compounded when governments sought to extract peasants' agricultural surplus through differential pricing policies and taxation. This was pursued in order to provide cheap food and raw materials to the emerging industrial centres. US food aid, during this period, further harmed Third World peasants' livelihoods.[38] The peasants could either accept the unfair prices they received for their produce or they could keep their produce and the government would feed the people using US Food Aid. US Food aid also had a less direct but even more devastating impact on their livelihoods, as explained in the next section.

37. McMichael, 2008:chapter 3
38. Bello, 2009: chapter 1

US Food Aid

As a result of subsidising its own agricultural production, the US developed a large wheat surplus, and sought to offload this onto allies in the Third World, as cheap or free food aid. The US chose to target this food aid toward countries that were geographically important in the battle against communism. Third World governments were encouraged to follow a cheap food policy as part of their drive toward industrialisation and hence they welcomed the imported grain. The problem was that this food aid undermined the prices that peasant producers could secure for their harvests. The price of wheat on world markets was significantly depressed by this transfer of subsidised food aid, so even when Third World governments did not receive food aid, imported wheat outcompeted the domestic production of indigenous staples. This led to large scale proletarianisation[39] of the peasantry throughout the Third World.[40]

In many cases, food aid was used as a powerful political and economic lever by the United States. At the 1974 World Food Conference in Rome, the US Secretary for Agriculture, Earl Butz, commented:

> I have heard ... that many people may become dependent on us for food. I know that was not supposed to be good news. To me, that was good news, because before people can do anything they have got to eat. And if you are looking for a way to get people to lean on you and be dependent on you, in terms of their co-operation with you, it seems to me that food dependence would be terrific.[41]

An example of Butz's optimistic assessment came about in the same year, when a 'man-made famine' in Bangladesh resulted in the deaths of between 27,000 and 100,000 people. At the time Bangladesh had a left-wing government, led by Shaikh Mujib,

---

39. Proletarianisation: The process whereby formerly subsistence agricultural producers are forced into the wage economy through the destruction of their livelihood.
40. Bello, 2009:chapter?????
41. quoted in Hayter, 1990:8

which the United States administration wanted to remove. The country was also heavily dependent on US food aid. In the midst of serious flooding that had ruined Bangladesh's harvest, two major food shipments to Bangladesh were cancelled by US commercial grain exporters. There are certainly unanswered questions as to whether this was at the behest of the US government.

As the famine began to unfold, the US refused to reinstate food shipments. Instead, it entered into a bargaining process with the government, forcing it to change its investment policies to promote the private sector and private enterprise. It also insisted that Bangladesh curtail its exports to Soviet Cuba, before it would agree to provide food shipments. The delay to food shipments that was caused by this action led directly to the famine that claimed so many lives. There are certainly questions as to whether the aim was to politically destabilise Bangladesh to the point where the government would be removed. That political transition came about when Shaikh Mujib was assassinated and his most pro-Western colleague took his place.[42] The opportunistic use of a man-made famine to force political control was reminiscent of the kind of control measures used by Joseph Stalin – surely not the impression that developed governments would like to be presented to their electorate?

Aid for Integrated Rural Development and the Green Revolution: the 1970s
Import Substitution Industrialisation caused alienation of the peasantry. This alienation, in turn, resulted in a growth in support for peasant based revolutionary socialist movements in many parts of the developing world. In order to contain these movements the US supported land reform in Taiwan and South Korea. This led to a level of peasant prosperity that allowed these countries to set their post war industrialisation in motion.[43] However, similar support for land reform as a counter-revolutionary tactic failed in Chile and Argentina, where the left came to power in the early 1970s. Consequently the World Bank and the US Agency for

42. Hayter, 1990:86-87
43. Bello, 2009:28

International Development (USAID) which administered the US bilateral aid budget altered their policies.

The new policy was to support the 'productivity of the poor' through support for the Green Revolution technology and practice in underdeveloped countries. The Green Revolution technology, which the World Bank now supported through loans and grants, included the use of specially designed High Yielding Variety (HYV) seeds, irrigation, and chemical fertilisers to produce wheat and rice. The use of these inputs led to significantly higher yields. The officially stated intention was to provide the poor with a stake in the state's economy. Such a stake would encourage them to identify their interests with the continuation of the capitalist state formation, rather than with revolutionary socialist movements.[44]

The World Bank did not want to challenge the richer sectors in rural areas. It did, however, want to avert revolutionary political movements amongst the poor. As Robert McNamara, the World Bank president outlined, in 1974:

> [Rural development] puts primary emphasis not on the redistribution of income and wealth – as justified as that may be in our member countries – but rather on increasing the productivity of the poor, thereby providing for the equitable sharing of the benefits of growth.[45]

A new rural development strategy, known as Integrated Rural Development, was promoted by donors as the means for 'rolling out' the Green Revolution technology and practice. It involved mobilising rural development projects through Third World states' central administration. This involved planning units and coordination committees at all levels of society. Experts from donor countries were employed at every level of these schemes. The belief was that central planning, led by the donor in co-operation with the domestic state, could effectively target the needs of the poor.[46] In Africa, state led agricultural development had some

---

44. Bello, 2009:chapter 1
45. Quoted in Bello, 2009:29
46. Degnbol-Martinussen and Engberg-Pedersen, 2003:45-47

positive outcomes, in boosting production and modernising agriculture.[47] India has not experienced a famine in more than 60 years, arguably as an outcome of the higher aggregate yields that the country has achieved through the Green Revolution.[48] However, the Green Revolution entailed specific incentives and economic outcomes that led to further impoverishment of the rural poor.

Many peasants, in India in particular, became impoverished through failed attempts to invest in the new technologies and increased proletarianisation which kept wages low.[49] Furthermore, the new technology favoured the development of labour-displacing mechanisation. This led to the concentration of landholdings into fewer hands.[50] Many poor peasants who could not afford the inputs found that they could not compete with wealthier farmers who could. Higher yields benefited wealthier farmers, as those who could not afford the new technologies suffered from the decline in prices that technology brought about. Those with larger landholdings accrued the greatest surplus as a result of this new technology, increasing inequality. Consequently, there was an increase in landlessness and poverty among peasants in many parts of the Third World. It should be noted that the Green Revolution never became firmly embedded in sub-Saharan Africa, to the extent that it did in Latin America and South Asia. Where it did make its presence known, very poor peasant farmers

47. Bello, 2009:69-70
48. However, it must be pointed out that Amartya Sen (1981) has shown, in his classic text, *Poverty and Famines: an essay on entitlement and famines*, that the Bengal Famine of 1942 (India's last famine) was not caused by a lack of food availability, but in fact took place in the context of a 'boom' harvest year. He shows in this text that mortality during famines is due to the inability of the poor to purchase, produce or otherwise access sufficient food, rather than a lack of food availability. However, this does not negate the possibility that a collapse in food availability, at the aggregate level, could trigger the economic circumstances in which a famine could take place, according to Sen. As a result of his analysis, famines are now correctly understood as economic and man-made, rather than natural, catastrophes.
49. Das, 2002:59
50. Ellis, 1992:177

were adversely affected because many of the higher yielding varieties relied heavily on chemicals, strictly balanced artificial fertilisers, pesticides and herbicides, which were sourced from donor
states. The cost of these drove many out of business. The machin-
ery necessary to use these expensive chemicals effectively could
only be purchased by more prosperous farmers, or through state
intervention. Governments, in this way, once again looked after
those whom they favoured. The outcome for the very poor could
have been an unforeseen consequence of a genuine attempt to
improve their lives, as some have suggested. However if that was
the case, one must ask why donor countries have not acted more
forcefully in an effort to put right this 'mistake'?

The Green Revolution did not challenge inequality in rural
areas. Rather it reinforced it. Overall, state-led, donor backed
efforts to increase the productivity of the poor failed. It could be
hypothesised that the creation of a new rural elite was facilitated
by the growth of a reactionary social class in rural areas. Such a
grouping was well placed to fight against revolutionary peasant
movements. This elite class could undermine the growing movement towards the politics of the left. If the growing move towards
socialist policies was contained or eradicated by local people, that
was one less socialist concern to contend with. By consolidating
landholdings, introducing mechanisation and commodifying the
input regime of much Third World agriculture, the Green Revolution
succeeded in creating the conditions through which multi-national
agrifood corporations could dramatically enhance the profitability
of their operations in the Third World.

When the debt crisis occurred in the late 1970s, the World Bank
was quick to blame the over involvement of the state in Third
World countries' development projects as the cause of their economic crises. It failed to accept the obvious explanation that the
economic shock of spiralling oil prices and interest rates had
thrown poor countries' balance sheets out of line. The debt crisis
provided the IFIs and bilateral donors with an ideal opportunity
to force a new orthodoxy on poor countries, one in which government intervention in the economy was reduced.

The Role of Aid in the Rise of Neoliberal Economic Policies: the 1980s

The administration of Margaret Thatcher in the UK and Ronald Regan in the US ushered in a new era in economic policy, referred to as neoliberalism. This 'project' was promoted with ideological fervour in the early 1980s, and ever since then its ideology and policy prescriptions have come to dominate decisions on aid allocation among donor states. These policies have played a major part in deepening inequality and poverty in the Third World, and in concentrating wealth in the hands of elites in underdeveloped countries.[51] For the moment it is enough to cite Harvey,[52] who has described the rise of neoliberal policies as a political project by the global capitalist elite. This project, he argues, represents an attempt to concentrate wealth in their own hands and hence promote their own power. The chosen mechanism he identifies is the extracting of tribute from poor countries. On this assessment, such a development should be considered a new phase in imperialism.

The economic policies employed are those which promote the role of markets, private enterprise and the global free mobility of capital at the expense of the involvement of the state in the economy. Part of this new approach directed heavily indebted countries to focus on exporting a limited range of commodities onto world markets and to rely on global markets for most of their needs. This contrasted sharply with the earlier focus on industrialising behind protective tariff barriers in order to become less reliant on imports. A standard set of policy prescriptions, in keeping with these Western economic ideologies, were forced on underdeveloped countries. ODA payments, and debt restructuring in particular, were conditional on their implementation.

The Third World debt crisis, that began in the late 1970s and continued until the mid-1980s, provided donor countries with a perfect opportunity to remodel the economies of countries in need of debt rescheduling, along these lines. From the early 1980s, conditions began to be attached to aid and debt rescheduling that demanded that poor countries drastically reordered their econ-

51. see chapter 6
52. 2005

omic and social policies. Aid donors expanded the role of aid at this time from promoting particular projects to transforming the entire state apparatus and economic policies of recipient countries. The term Structural Adjustment Policies (SAPs) was used to refer to this process.

The SAPs promoted by the Washington based institutions of the World Bank, IMF and US Treasury came to be known as the 'Washington Consensus'. Their implementation became the dominant goal of ODA throughout the 1980s and 1990s. Glennie[53] has summarised what he terms the '10 Commandments of the Washington Consensus'. These are:

Tighten government spending across the board.
Redirect public expenditure to support growth and pro-poor services.
Tax reform (lower marginal rates and a broader tax base).
Market determined interest rates.
Competitive exchange rates to induce growth in exports.
Reducing trade barriers.
Reducing government controls over foreign investment.
The privatisation of state owned industries and service provision.
Reducing regulation governing competition.
Legally enforcing property rights.

A key outcome of these economic policies has been the globalisation of production and consumption. This has provided opportunities for the wealthy nations to reap previously unimaginable profits at the expense of the poor.[54] Such has been the impact of these policies over the last three decades, that Glennie[55] equates the question 'has aid led to growth?' with the question 'has a neoliberal economic agenda led to growth?'

---

53. 2008:38
54. The mechanisms by which this has taken place will be expanded upon in chapter 6.
55. 2008:81

The Debt Crisis

African governments began to incur huge foreign debts from as early as the 1960s, as they sought to fund infrastructural development.[56] Oil prices quadrupled in the mid-1970s, an intended result of OPEC countries' decision to limit the supply of oil onto world markets. Western banks were inundated with 'petro-dollars' from oil producing states and sought opportunities to lend these new funds. The banks induced Third World states to borrow from them through offering concessional interest rates. Monetary policy in the United States underwent a transformation between 1979 and 1981. During that time the chairman of the US Federal Reserve increased interest rates from near zero to close to 20%.[57] This sudden spike in interest rates, accompanied by increasing global commodity market price volatility, forced economies throughout the Global South into crisis. Mexico was the first state to default on its debt repayments in 1982. This was quickly followed by a domino effect of other countries defaulting.

The creditor banks were faced with an immediate crisis as a result of underdeveloped countries' inability to repay their loans. The global financial system was faced with potential collapse. Many of the biggest banks had lent several multiples of their capital base to poor countries, that were unable to service that debt.[58] When short term debt was taken into account, Argentina's debt service ratio was 179% of export earnings, Mexico's was 129%, Brazil's was 122% and Chile's was 116%. Given that the Development Assistance Committee (DAC), which governs development policy amongst donors, considered a debt servicing ratio of 20 per cent of export earnings to indicate a 'danger level', the extent of the crisis becomes clear.[59]

The US Treasury, and the IMF, resolved the crisis by allowing indebted countries to reschedule their debt repayments. The offer of assistance in this regard was accompanied by an insistence that these countries implement a wide range of institutional and policy reforms reflecting the new western, free market agenda. Debtor

56. Schoepf *et al*, 2000:97
57. Harvey, 2005:27-29
58. Hayter and Watson, 1985:25
59. Ibid:23-24

governments had to secure IMF approval in order to receive any future ODA and debt rescheduling. This forced debtor governments to slash their budget deficits in order to enable them to repay their loans. They were forced to cut wages, imports, investment, food subsidies and social spending in order to repay the high interest on their debt. They were forced to privatise state owned industries, introduce legal changes to make labour markets more flexible and devalue their currencies in order to promote exports.[60] In Mexico as many as four million people lost their jobs in the immediate aftermath of these policy changes. In Brazil, the IMF demanded that wages be reduced by 20% between 1981 and 1982. This had the effect of increasing the numbers of those earning less than half the official minimum wage, by a third, to 10 million. Many people in Brazil resorted to raiding supermarkets for basic food stuffs.[61]

In Africa, the World Bank linked further loans to the willingness of governments to accept policy reform. The Bank instructed African governments to devalue their currencies, to privatise government enterprises and public services, as well as to provide concessions to foreign capital such as tax incentives, the free repatriation of profits and the elimination of tariff protection for domestic businesses. It further directed them to end minimum wages and labour protections.[62] This policy departure on the part of the IFIs has been described as their transformation into 'centres for the propagation and enforcement of "free market fundamentalism" and neoliberal orthodoxy'.[63]

The austerity measures forced on underdeveloped countries by the IFIs were not in the interests of their own economies or their peoples. These policies intentionally shifted the burden of bailing out the northern banks from the tax-payers in the North onto the poor in the Third World. In the longer term, these policies have enriched the wealthy Western elite at the expense of the poor in the Third World.[64]

60. Harvey, 2005:29
61. Hayter and Watson, 1985:29
62. Schoepf et al, 2000:99
63. 2005:25
64. see chapter 6

In the mid-1980s, the World Bank's lending practices served as the model for other multilateral lending institutions.[65] This continues to be the case today. In the early 1980s, a quarter of ODA was channelled through these multilateral institutions. The remaining three quarters took the form of direct bilateral aid. A little over half of all DAC members' aid at this time was 'tied' to the purchase of goods or services from the donor countries. Much of this aid was included in funding for particular projects. 'General non-project assistance', which included loans and grants to pay for the import of specified goods and services, balance of payments and budget support, accounted for 15% of aid flows, with debt relief accounting for another 3%. The conditions attached to this non-project assistance were used as a vehicle for imposing the SAP reforms on underdeveloped countries. In subsequent years this type of lending increased in importance relative to project assistance.

The most significant outcome of ODA developments in the 1980s and 1990s was that the Washington based IFIs, in tandem with the US Treasury, increasingly used aid to dictate economic and social policy formation in poor countries. Looking at (sub-Saharan) African policy choices and economic structures today, compared with those at the start of the 1980s, it is clear that most African countries have changed very significantly along the lines of the so-called 'Washington Consensus'.[67] The same is true, generally, for countries throughout the Third World, or Global South as it has come to be known.

At a time when they could least afford it, when they were at their most vulnerable, developing countries were forced to accept crippling changes that would shift many more millions into poverty and ensure the servitude of the developing nations to the Western powers for generations to come. Offsetting a small increase in taxes in developed nations, by squeezing even more money from those people who have nothing, has left a legacy of poverty and suffering. That those same policies continue to the present

65. Hayter (1985:12-13)
66. Ibid: 13-15
67. Glennie (2008: 37)

day, and have even been strengthened in some cases, is a guilt that should weigh heavily on the conscience of Western governments. By implication, this is a shame on the people who vote these governments into power.

The Aid Regime in the 2000s:
A 'New Aid Architecture' or more of the same?
In the 1990s aid came to play a crucial role in enabling developed countries to restructure underdeveloped countries' economies in ways that they deemed favourable. However, the 1990s were also a time of crisis for aid generally. A decade of intense structural adjustment lending reached a peak in 1990. At this time, the cold war came to an end and a major part of the rationale for giving aid evaporated. Developed countries no longer needed to provide aid to poor countries in order to win support against the Soviet Union. There was a decade of declining aid flows, both in real terms, and as a percentage of developed country GNI.[68] By 1997 aid flows to Africa were back to 1983 levels.[69] However, it was not long before renewed calls for more aid to poor countries emerged. This led to a new era of aid optimism, with new official goals and targets for aid, in the 2000s.

The United Nations Millennium Summit in 2000 played a large part in ushering in this 'new era' in aid. The Millennium Development Goals (MDGs) were agreed at this meeting – the largest gathering of world leaders in history.[70] The 147 assembled leaders adopted a global statement, the Millennium Declaration, which committed the states of the world to a global development project.[71] The project set the MDGs.[72]

A consensus has developed amongst donors that the promotion of economic growth in underdeveloped countries is the means by which these goals will be met. This approach asserts that for economic growth in the poorest countries to be achieved,

68. see chapter 3
69. Glennie, 2008:11
70. Sachs, 2005, p 210
71. Ibid, p 211
72. see chapter 1

unprecedented levels of ODA are required. As Woodward and Simms[73] put it, 'Poverty reduction, according to the orthodoxy, requires rapid economic growth in developing countries; economic growth in developing economies in turn requires rapid growth in the global economy: therefore poverty reduction requires the fastest possible growth in the global economy'. A huge literature has developed debating the role that aid can play in stimulating economic growth in underdeveloped countries and the role that economic growth in underdeveloped countries plays in poverty reduction. Orthodox accounts argue that aid does promote growth and poverty reduction.[74]

For the moment, it is enough to observe that the promotion of global economic growth is something from which those with access to and control of capital can expect disproportionate benefit relative to the poor. It is also perfectly possible for economic growth to occur and for the poor to miss out on any of the benefit. Indeed, growth along liberalised economic lines has been shown to provide few benefits to the poor.[75]

Accompanying this new optimism for aid is a new body of thinking that seeks to blame poor country governments for the historical failure of their countries to develop. The World Bank has been vocal in its calls for 'good governance', the fight against corruption and the establishment of liberal democratic institutions of governance. This approach appealed to the Bank because it diverted attention from the damaging role that the imposition of donor-led Structural Adjustment had played over preceding decades.[76] With poor countries' economies thoroughly liberalised by the late 1990s, the IFIs sought out new areas of influence over poor states, expanding their influence into the political realm. This emerged as a recognition that global finance requires a stable political context within which to operate. Government protection of property rights is essential for such markets to flourish.

---

73. 2006
74. Chapter 7 will provide a critical response to this viewpoint, and will show that it is a baseless argument, both in theory and fact.
75. Woodward and Simms, 2006
76. Boas and McNeill, 2003:68-69

The new approach calls for underdeveloped country governments to practise 'good governance', to combat corruption and to
develop their 'capacity' to design and implement policy and carry
out other functions. The overarching Western economic agenda
still applies within this new focus on the political realm. The state
is still expected to be small and to function primarily as a facilit-
ator of the private sector. However, it is expected to be efficient in
how it does this.[77] Unsurprisingly, a new regime of aid conditionalities emerged to promote this new agenda. Between 1995 and
1999, public sector governance conditions accounted for 17% of
World Bank loan conditions. By 2007 these accounted for 50%.[78]

Accompanying calls for good governance are calls for poor
countries to 'own' development policies. This requires that all levels
of society to be involved in formulating development policy, and
therefore in building the capacity of civil society, to participate in
this process. IFIs require that aid recipient countries develop
'Poverty Reduction Strategy Papers (PRSPs)' in consultation with
civil society groups. In practice, this process has not led to ownership of development policy by recipient countries. It has merely
provided a facade of recipient country and civil society particip-
ation. Governments in developing countries were acting as ad-
ministrators of donor nations' policies. These governments are little
more than managers working on behalf of donor nations in much
the same way as puppet monarchies and governments helped to
administer colonial rule in bygone years.

Of the 20 countries to complete a PRSP by 2003, 16 had received
IMF loans approved prior to their completion. Their own independent evaluation committees found that loans from the IFIs
informed their PRSPs, rather than the other way around.[79] The
World Bank grades PRSPs, indicating the degree to which it
approves of the policies contained in them. This runs counter to
the stated rationale of the exercise.[80] Another common criticism is
that the PRSPs contain such a large range of policy proposals that

---

77. Ibid
78. Glennie, 2008:50
79. Glennie, 2008:47
80. Ibid

the donors can simply pick and choose which policies to support. In Zambia, rather than increasing democratic accountability, the PRSP process largely undermined it. The political parties and their elected representatives were not invited to participate in formulating the document. Instead, unelected (and therefore unaccountable) civil society groups were given control of the process. This was an attempt to minimise the risk of the ability for derailment by political parties in the event of a change of government. The effect, however, was to undermine the democratic system in the country.[81]

Free market, liberal economics provided the major rationale for aid since the 1980s. This 'new aid architecture' of the early 21st century has not offered any genuine departure. It has merely couched the same level of control of poor country economic and social policy in 'softer' language and expanded this control into the political realm. Privatisation of state owned industries, for example, is considered to be an essential aspect of 'good governance'. 'Good governance' is generally promoted as a means of creating an enabling environment for foreign business interests. Corruption often increases the cost of doing business for MNCs in underdeveloped countries. Tackling and reducing corruption, therefore, as part of good governance, will enhance the possibility for these firms to accrue larger profits. Good governance also requires developing a predictable and enforceable system of property rights. This, again, is something that is in the interests of foreign businesses operating in aid recipient countries. There is very little point in a Western business entering a developing country to set up a factory, power plant, or oil refinery if there is a possibility that they will lose control of it at some point in the future. Of course, one could argue that good governance also protects and supports emerging, indigenous businesses. This may be so, but it is only the wealthy who can afford such enterprise in resource starved economies. The real benefits accrue to Western enterprises.

---

81. Ibid, 65

Conclusion

It is important to separate the rhetoric and the reality of aid through the various phases in its development over the last century. From its earliest incarnation, ODA has been used to remodel under-developed countries' economies, in ways that benefit the donor states. Particular benefit has been enjoyed and experienced by the powerful and the wealthy elites in the donor states, and to a lesser extent, to their counterparts in the developed countries. From this perspective, it is clear that ODA has played the part of facilitating several phases of imperialism since the end of WWII. The next chapter explores how the current phase of imperialism, a whole-hearted commitment to economic growth, has created and sustained poverty in the underdeveloped regions of the world.

CHAPTER SIX

Aid, Economic Growth,
and the Creation of Poverty

Since the end of World War II 'aid has played' a central role in promoting imperialism throughout the world. The mechanisms of the economic agenda that believes growth is the cure for all ills have created and deepened poverty and inequality in the Third World. ODA has been an instrument of manipulation, in bringing about this new reality. The means by which this has occurred have been diverse.

Social spending decreases when governments are forced by donors to budget 'prudently'. Privatisation of service provision and state enterprises reduces access by the poor. The fallout of financial crises and deregulation heavily burden the poor. Poor country economies are impoverished by the effect of export orientation, and the associated effect of declining international terms of trade on the poor. Agreements negotiated at the World Trade Organisation (WTO) promote the interests of multi-national corporations (MNCs) *vis-à-vis* third world economies. The pursuit of monetarist policies and low inflation has enabled the rich to become richer at the expense of the poor. The conditions attached to aid have played a large part in birthing all of these negative outcomes. All these negative effects on poor countries and poor people in those countries must be seen as the principal outcome of aid dependency in the Global South over the last 30 years.

These policies have ensured that the Global South is beholden to the Global North in all areas of government and development. The Darwinian ideology of survival of the fittest, as exercised through 'free markets', has been operated in a completely unjust manner. The established mechanisms will ensure that the Global South always remains 'unfit': forever at a disadvantage when competing with nations in the Global North. Whenever a financial crisis hits the world the nations in the Global South are always hit hardest. In the guise of ODA, the developed nations can use an economic crisis to consolidate their hold on the underdeveloped nations. In such times of turmoil the wealthy developed countries often take advantage of the underdeveloped nations by subjecting them to ever more convoluted and devastating methods of exploitation.

Reduced Social Expenditure

From the early 1980s, Structural Adjustment Policies (SAPs) were enforced by the IMF on heavily indebted poor countries. These countries had to earn the IMF's stamp of approval in order to receive ODA or debt rescheduling. The rules imposed included strict fiscal discipline, reducing government spending on health, education and infrastructure. SAPs were imposed on 42 countries in the 1980s and 1990s as a condition for receiving new loans.[1] The system ensures that the rich nations will always get what is owed to them regardless of the effect this has on the nations of the Global South. Financial ruin and mass starvation are often the local end result. The question to be explored can be framed as: what effect have these cuts in social expenditure had on poverty in poor countries?

Zaire provides a good example of the direct impact of SAPs on public service provision. The previous chapter mentioned the degree to which President Mobutu had corruptly embezzled a sizeable proportion of the money advanced to the country. In 1983, strict IMF and World Bank conditions were placed on the country's social expenditure in order to enable it to repay this debt. Little, if any, consideration was given to the human cost of this requirement. Neither did it consider the fact that the people who were now being made to suffer had already suffered when the loan money was stolen in the first place by Mobutu. The government sharply reduced the budget for social services, raising user fees for health services and education. In 1984, more than 80,000 teachers and health workers were dismissed from their

---

1. Schoepf *et al*, 2000:92

positions in a further bid to cut government expenditure.[2] Clearly, this had a direct impact on the poor in Zaire, denying many access to healthcare and education. The developed nations allowed this to happen. It was the easiest way for them to get their money back. School children and the ill in the developing world were really not in any position to offer troublesome resistance.

This pattern was repeated throughout the underdeveloped world in the 1980s. Overall, in Sub-Saharan Africa, government spending on education dropped by 65% in the period 1980 to 1987.[3] By 1995, twenty-eight out of thirty-seven countries in the region had introduced fees for basic healthcare, denying access to the poorest people.[4] Increased user fees in Kenya, Zambia, Madagascar, Tanzania and Senegal led to a decline in the use of maternity and basic healthcare services amongst the poorest, and led directly to increases in infant mortality and maternal health risks.[5] In Zimbabwe, the introduction of user fees led to a 25% reduction in access to health facilities and a corresponding 13% rise in child mortality.[6] Cutbacks in state provision were accompanied by the privatisation of service provision, partly as another means of limiting social expenditure by the state. This could only affect the poor in a negative way.

Privatisation of Service Provision
Mike Obadan[7] notes, 'Privatisation and commercialisation have been central components of the SAPs foisted by the World Bank on indebted Third World countries.' Over 100 countries, on every continent, have privatised some or all of their industries. In sub-Saharan Africa, by 2002, 3,486 privatisation transactions had taken place, generating an income to states of $6.7 billion.[8] In his review of the literature analysing the effects of privatisation in underdeveloped countries, Obadan notes that, in theory, privatis-

---

2. Schoepf *et al*, 2000:92-94
3. Glennie, 2008:42-44
4. Ibid
5. Ibid
6. Ibid
7. 2008:21
8. Ibid, 43

ation can result in greater efficiency, productivity and profitability for state owned enterprises that are privatised. However, he also observes that state owned enterprises may have objectives other than profit. If service provision becomes the focus it is reasonable to assume that profitability may increase in the case of privatisation. Obadan also notes that where the purchaser of a state owned enterprise is a foreign interest, privatisation can result in greater international inequality, due to the export of profits from poor countries.[9] Privatisation is often a double-edged sword. The funds generated from the privatisation of an industry may be immediately claimed by countries in the Global North as loan repayments. If the privatised industry enters foreign hands, as is often the case, many of the profits generated by the industry leave the country, with only a small percentage being funnelled back into the industry as investment. When countries privatise health service it is important for hospitals and clinics to offer the best possible service. If they don't, the sick will go elsewhere. In these circumstances, service providers are strongly motivated to ensure that a significant percentage of the profits that they generate are ploughed back in to improving the service that they offer. In poor nations, choice is limited to begin with. When privatisation places the small number of health services in the hands of multinational organisations they have no real motivation for improving the health services that they provide. The role played by MNCs compounds the impact of privatisation on the poor in underdeveloped countries.

Madeley has highlighted that MNCs have been involved, as the private interest, in many instances of privatisation throughout the Third World.[10] For example, in Argentina, 60% of the state assets sold by 1995 had been purchased by foreign investors from just 19 countries.[11] Deregulation of controls on the activities of MNCs, another aspect of SAPs, enables them to repatriate their profits from the countries where they operate. When they don't have to pay tax they place a further drain on the domestic countries'

9. Ibid, 53
10. 1999:18-20
11. Ibid

resources. MNCs may also obtain a windfall profit, as state assets are often sold off at prices that undervalue their true worth. This creates an incentive for MNCs to engage in asset stripping of formerly state owned operations in order to realise this windfall profit. This type of situation can occur when corrupt kick-backs to government politicians are involved. It has been observed that, 'privatisation and commercialisation ... on the whole ... have been designed to meet the needs of transnational business in a fast globalising market'.[12]

Mike Obadan[13] highlights several ways that privatisation can harm the poor. He draws attention to increased unemployment (when privatised enterprises seek to reduce production costs). He also points out the reduction of services including essential healthcare, education, electricity and water, in poor disadvantaged rural areas. The creation of unemployment through privatisation is a particularly acute problem given the high rates of unemployment in underdeveloped countries generally. Employment in the state sector in Mexico was cut in half between 1988 and 1994. Interestingly, the number of state owned firms fell from 1,100 in 1982 to 200 by 1994. These two sources of unemployment combined to create a situation of mass unemployment and crisis in Mexican cities, which were transformed into some of the most dangerous places on earth.[14] Another result of privatisation in Mexico was the creation of billionaires. Of the 24 new billionaires that the country's economic restructuring brought about, 17 had participated in purchasing state owned firms.[15]

Generally when private companies assume responsibility for the delivery of essential services, the focus of delivery is towards those who can afford to pay. The poor become excluded because they cannot pay increased user charges. The privatisation of water provision, widespread in recent years, often results in people in rural areas being denied access to clean water. It is often simply unprofitable for a privatised water company to provide water to

12. Martin (1993), in Obadan, 2008:14
13. 2008:54
14. Harvey, 2005:98-104
15. Ibid

rural areas, since the infrastructure costs are high and poor people cannot afford to pay the fees.[16] Privatisation of healthcare in Zimbabwe was responsible for the re-emergence of TB and cholera in the country.[17] Because poor people could not afford fees for privatised healthcare, diseases that had almost been eradicated re-emerged. At the same time, unemployment rose dramatically because cheap, subsidised US food imports flooded the market and undercut staple food prices. This caused a flood of peasants to the cities in search of work when they could no longer compete with subsidised prices. That this should be allowed to happen raises questions concerning the benevolence of the Global North. The effects of a privatised healthcare on the very poor is easy to anticipate, and the fact that no provision is made for the very poor when healthcare is privatised is more than just an unforeseen consequence. Decisions that deny access by millions of the world's poorest people to healthcare are made in cold and calculating ways through policies that are drafted by policy makers in the Global North and executed by officials in the Global South.

The Gendered Effects of Structural Adjustment

Poverty increasingly affects women more than men in underdeveloped countries.[18] It has been widely recognised that SAPs have a gendered impact, that is to say that women and men experienced the effects differently in countries in which these policies were implemented. The following extract summarises the findings of a USAID report on the gendered impact of SAPs:

> One recent study conducted for … USAID …indicates that stabilisation and adjustment policies have had five primary negative consequences for women. First, evidence everywhere demonstrates that poverty is increasingly gendered. The so-called 'feminisation of poverty' is particularly acute among female-headed households and elderly women. Second, women have acted as 'shock absorbers' during adjustment by curtailing their own consumption and increasing

16. Hemson, 2008:13-46
17. Madeley (1999: 19)
18. see chapter 2

their workload to compensate for household income loss. Third, women tend to be more directly affected by reductions in social welfare spending and public programmes. Privatisation and welfare cuts often simply mean that social services are shifted from the paid to the unpaid labour of women. Fourth, gains made toward the goal of gender equality during the 1970s are being eroded due to shifts in the employment market and reductions in child care, education and retraining programmes. Finally, public expenditure constraints have a direct impact on women's employment and working conditions due to the relatively high representation of women in public sector occupations.[19]

It is often observed that SAPs shifted the burden of adjustment to the debt crisis onto the poor in underdeveloped countries. What the above quote shows is that SAPs shifted the burden of adjustment onto the poor, and *poor women in particular*, in underdeveloped countries. This goes a long way to explaining the increasing feminisation of poverty in the Global South.[20] The extract bears testimony to the fact that the Global North is fully aware of the problems being created by their policies towards the Global south, especially in the lives of women. Recognising the problem is only the first step. Unfortunately the step that really matters, that of changing the unfair policies that are creating the problems in the first place, has yet to be taken.

Global Financial Deregulation
ODA has played a part in the rise of global financial deregulation. Deregulation has facilitated the rise to power of a powerful financial elite. Financialisation has been the principle means by which this elite class procured and concentrated its wealth since the advent of the free market economics.[21] The World Trade Organisation (WTO), established in 1995, has been the principal forum where this has been achieved. The WTO ostensibly creates a set of rules governing how much countries can protect or subsidise particular

19. Brodie, 1994:49-50
20. as observed in chapter 2
21. Harvey, 2005:87-119

industries. It includes a judiciary, controlled by Northern states, that enforces the rules, and a forum to which countries return recurrently to update the rules.[22] In practice, it has been the primary vehicle by which developed countries have achieved the global deregulation of markets, including financial markets. This has formed the foundation on which US, European and Japanese financial capital has been able to exact tribute from the rest of the world, often through the management of currency crises.

Immense pressure is often wielded by aid donors on aid recipient states, in negotiations at the WTO, through threats to withdraw ODA or debt relief.[23] By way of recent example, the European Union (EU) Trade Commissioner explicitly linked future EU aid decisions to the agreement to Economic Partnership Agreements by aid recipient states at the WTO.[24] Aid, used instrumentally in this way, has proven to be remarkably effective in these negotiations.

It is widely recognised that financial deregulation, and the consequent ballooning of financial speculation, played a central role in bringing about the current global economic crisis. There has been an ever increasing number of currency crises for as long as deregulation of financial and capital markets has been pursued. These crises have often had extraordinarily detrimental effects on poor people, as their effects have spilled over to the real economy.

It is universally recognised that financial deregulation allows financial crises to spread around the world at a dramatic rate, through what is known as a contagion effect. Even the US Federal Reserve chairman, Alan Greenspan, speaking after the onset of the Asian crisis in 1998, observed that: 'Efficient global financial markets ... facilitate the transmission of financial distortions with greater speed and more efficiently than ever.'[25]

Financialisation of the global economy has occurred against the backdrop of a long period of declining profits from productive investment and declining productivity of capital. As the twentieth century progressed, fewer and fewer productive investment

22. Weis, 2007:128
23. Boas and McNeill, 2003:42-43
24. Glennie, 2008:135
25. quoted in Dehesa, 2006:121

opportunities presented themselves to the financial elite. They therefore sought to deregulate financial markets around the world so they could invest in speculation, as an alternative means of securing profit. Like modern day versions of conquering generals, these individuals drew up battle plans to take control of as large a portion of the earth's resources as they could grab. Financialisation in the global economy has replaced the association of monetary capital to the real economy, with the association of credit (based on future commodities produced by future labour) to financial markets.[26] By the mid-1990s, the financial economy as a whole managed 50 times more money than the real economy. Of that money in the financial economy, a sizeable proportion lay in the hands of a very small number of institutions and individual investors. These individuals and organisations are the real global powerbrokers.

The Indian stock market, the largest in the Global South, is only one thirtieth the size of the US stock market. The Nigerian stock market is the second largest in Sub-Saharan Africa, but is only one five thousandth the size of the US stock market.[27] When 'hot' money flows into these countries' markets, it can drive up financial and asset bubbles extremely quickly, since the quantities of funds can be so vastly out of proportion to the size of their markets. As soon as these economies face any trouble, the resulting capital flight massively accentuates the down turn. Finance capital behaves pro-cyclically. It enters the economy at the wrong time, distorting an already overheating economy. It also leaves at the wrong time, creating capital flight at just the time when the market needs all of the liquidity it can get.[28] The virtually unlimited mobility of financial capital, the herd mentality of investors and the diverse portfolios of investment funds, allowed the Mexican 'tequila crisis' of 1995 to spread almost immediately to Brazil and Argentina, with devastating consequences. It also spread to and affected Chile, Thailand, the Philippines and Poland.[29]

26. Dierckxsens, 2000:41-60
27. Chang, 2007:87
28. Ibid
29. Harvey, 2005:94

The Mexican crisis of 1995 was sparked, as had been the debt crisis in 1982, by the raising of interest rates in the US. There was a consequential run on the Mexican currency, as investors recognised that Mexico would be crippled by the burden of increased interest payments. Investors predicted that devaluation would be required. The resulting speculative pressure on the peso did indeed lead to devaluation, resulting in massive profits for many speculators. That the sentiment of investors, volatile enough in a normal market climate, can have such an immediate and devastating effect on a country's economy has the effect of scaring off much legitimate investment. That the markets and currency in countries like Mexico can be influenced so easily ensures that it remains a popular target for those who make profits from currency speculation. This is nothing short of an international smash and grab that the country is powerless to prevent, not least because of conditions imposed on it because of aid.[30]

Mexico had been issuing dollar denominated debt up to this point. Domestic businesses were faced with an inability to repay this debt, since they had borrowed in dollars and were now attempting to repay the debt in pesos that had lost their value. The resulting credit crunch cost Mexico dearly in terms of unemployment and poverty, as many businesses went bankrupt. On the other hand, the devaluation provided opportunity for US investors. They had already made a windfall profit through speculating on, and therefore bringing about, the devaluation, now they could rush in and buy up almost the entire Mexican banking system. The result was a huge flow of tribute to the US financial elite.[31]

The collapse of a speculative property market bubble in Thailand in 1997 led to the devaluation of its currency, and spread almost immediately to Indonesia, Malaysia and the Philippines. From there it spread to Hong Kong, Taiwan, Singapore and South Korea, before hitting Estonia, Russia and Brazil.[32] David Harvey argues that US Hedge Funds orchestrated the crisis. They bet against these economies on the one hand. On the other, they

30. See chapter 8 for a discussion on ways that this can be prevented
31. Harvey, 2005:98-104
32. Harvey, 2005:96

denied corporations based in these regions liquidity at a point of 'minor difficulty'.[33] As the Asian crisis began to take hold, the IMF insisted that interest rates payable should be raised and government spending slashed. This protected the interests of international creditors, but led to a deep recession.

The outcome of this crisis was a fourfold increase in unemployment in South Korea, a threefold increase in Thailand and a tenfold increase in Indonesia. In South Korea, a quarter of the population fell into poverty. Urban poverty tripled and total poverty doubled in Indonesia.[34] Another consequence was a huge flow of tribute to Wall Street, boosting the stock market at a time of declining savings in the US. When the affected economies began declaring bankruptcy, foreign direct investment flooded back in to buy up the 'perfectly viable companies' that had been left in ruins by the crash, reaping a windfall profit.[35]

The liberalisation of financial capital has been facilitated, in part, as this section has outlined, by donor countries using ODA as a strong lever in negotiations at the WTO. The consequence of this financial deregulation has been the massive flow of tribute to US and other financial interests, at the expense of poor people in underdeveloped countries. The IMF, the gatekeeper of ODA, has governed this process, acting in the interests of the creditors. The interests of the wealthy have been attended to at the expense of the poor.

The effects of Deflationary Policies in the South and their Effect on the Poor

A key aspect of the SAPs, imposed on countries in the South, was that they should mandate their central banks to keep inflation low. The IMF imposed this condition strictly in every instance. It has continued this practice in reacting to financial crises throughout the Global South. Pettifor describes the reason for this:

> Wall Street and the US government … use the IMF as an agent for implementing effectively deflationary policies, whose ulti-

33. Ibid
34. Chua, 2003, in Harvey, 2005:96
35. Ibid, 98

mate purpose is not to reduce poverty ... but always, and only, to protect the value of creditor assets.[36]

This has been achieved by mandating 'independent' central banks to keep inflation low, by raising interest rates to tackle inflation at all costs. Run-away inflation can harm the poor, as the value of their cash income can be wiped out. However, inflation can assist the poor if it accompanies economic growth from which they benefit. For the financial sector, on the other hand, led by global finance capital, high interest rates enhance the value of their investments. Ha-Joon Chang[37] has observed that 'independent' central banks are rarely independent, and pay more attention to the concerns of the financial sector than any other.

When interest rates are high, it becomes increasingly difficult for companies to access credit. Chang[38] cites the example of South Africa, which followed an IMF approved macroeconomic policy on achieving independence in 1994. This, he says, was considered necessary in order not to scare away investors given the ANC's revolutionary Marxist history. Interest rates were maintained at 10-12% in the 1990s and early 2000s.[39] Few firms could afford to borrow, given an average profit rate for firms of 6%. Growth and employment suffered greatly. Given the huge need for jobs and growth in underdeveloped countries required to tackle poverty, this had disastrous consequences for the poor. The official unemployment rate in South Africa rose to 26-28%, one of the highest levels in the world.[40] He points out that profit rates for firms outside the financial sector in underdeveloped countries are generally 3-7%. Interest rates above this level give an incentive for potential investors to put their money into bonds or into the bank. That's where they will get a higher rate of return. This again benefits the financial sector at the expense of jobs for the poor.[41] In these circumstances the powerful financial sector once again benefits at

36. Pettifor, 2001:43
37. 2007:152-158
38. 2007:152-158
39. Ibid
40. Ibid
41. Ibid

the expense of the rest of the economy. Yet it is only in the real economy that poverty can be addressed and reduced. Through the process of privatisation, wealthy Western elites have bought significant stakes in banks operating in under developed nations. They therefore prosper from the profits generated from higher interest rates and investment. As with other sectors, the gains made in this economic environment flow out of the poor country.

The IMF also insists that underdeveloped countries should balance their budgets and not engage in deficit spending. This too is deflationary. In reality, underdeveloped countries should be attempting to balance their budget across the economic cycle, rather than in an individual year.[42] If they followed this policy they would be able to run a budget surplus during times of economic growth, which could be reinvested in the economy during times of recession. It should also be noted that in underdeveloped economies the statistics for unemployment do not include extremely low paid informal sector employment. The real impact is, therefore, even greater. This would result in deficit spending during years of economic crisis, but in the long run it would be compensated for by a budget surplus in years of growth. Smoothing-out the economic cycle in this way would avoid the boom and bust cycle. These policies could enable countries to achieve greater long term growth, and hence tackle poverty. However, the IMF is primarily concerned that underdeveloped countries will continue to be able to repay external debt. The requirements for balanced budgets insulate creditors and do not address poverty.

The IMF forced Indonesia to cut government spending during its financial and economic crisis in 1997. As a result of this demand from the IMF, food subsidies were abolished and interest rates were increased to 80 %.[43] By early 1998, 100 firms went bankrupt every day and mass unemployment followed. All of this led to urban riots and a fall in output of 16% in 1998.[44] At the same time, the financial sector and international creditors were protected by the requirement for high interest rates and reduced government

---

42. Chang, 2007:155-158
43. Chang, 2007:156
44. Ibid

spending. It's obvious that the interests of global finance were prioritised above all else. A massive increase in poverty resulted. The burden of the crisis, from which speculative capital reaped huge rewards, was placed onto the poor. The power wielded by the IMF and the fear that it commands results in governments being forced into making decisions that isolate and exploit the poorest people in their countries. Protecting the interests of financial capital at all costs is the primary mandate. Developing nations are only too aware of the dire consequences of failing to meet that unjust obligation. The choices being faced by governments in the Global South each and every day are a matter of life and death. Effectively, they can either sacrifice the lives of tens of thousands today in order to appease wealthy interest groups or do the right thing and risk being classified as a pariah state. That will result in many more of their poorest citizens being sacrificed in the future. Every voter in every country of the Global North shares some responsibility for the continuation of this injustice.

The IMF's deflationary policies, forced on underdeveloped countries as part of the liberal, free market economic agenda, have reduced economic growth throughout the Global South. This has harmed the poor the most. It has denied poor countries the opportunity for economic growth that could reduce poverty. At the centre of this policy agenda, the promotion of finance capital is at the expense of the poor. Wherever IMF approval has been needed for underdeveloped countries to access ODA, these policies have been enforced. Although indirect, these effects of aid are severe. They trap poor countries into low growth, high unemployment economic cycles, from which they cannot escape.

Export Orientation and the poor
Pursuit of the free trade economic agenda forces underdeveloped countries to rely on exporting to world markets those products in which they have a perceived 'comparative advantage' of production, onto world markets. They have to import all of the other products that they require. Wholesale tariff reduction has been a condition on receiving ODA throughout the South. Agreements made at the WTO, where the threat to withdraw aid has often been

used as leverage, have furthered the promotion of global markets. This has opened up underdeveloped countries' economies to world trade and forced them to compete in international markets. Many economies are ill equipped to function in such markets. This leaves them at a disadvantage compared to businesses operating out of the Global North. Underdeveloped countries have increasingly become dependent on exporting a limited number of agricultural commodities to developed countries, as this is the area where it is supposed that they have a 'comparative advantage'. This has contributed to poverty creation in these regions, through the fostering of unequal exchange between the Global North and Global South.

Reductions in tariffs by underdeveloped countries had an important direct and negative impact on their fiscal position, since many of these countries relied on import tariffs. During the period of Import Substitution Industrialisation these tariffs were a source of revenue. Poor countries rely heavily on tariffs as they find it hard to generate alternative sources of revenue. Indeed some of the poorest countries rely on tariffs for more than 50% of total government revenue.[45] In low income countries, which have been forced to reduce tariffs, less than 30% of the revenue lost due to trade liberalisation over the last 25 years, has been replaced with other sources.[46] This has left the poorest countries with major shortages of funds for social provision. Reduction in tariffs has therefore left them more dependent on aid as a source of revenue than before.

According to the economic theory utilised, all countries that engage in world trade will benefit from it. The assumption is that there will be no attempt to introduce tariffs or subsidies that distort the market. Countries should therefore focus on producing those products for which they have a relative comparative factor advantage. The factors of production are land, labour and capital. Since labour and land are relatively abundant and capital less so in underdeveloped countries, it is thought that in a free market, underdeveloped countries will focus their efforts on producing labour and land intensive goods. Such goods are generally agri-

---

45. Chang, 2007:69
46. Ibid

cultural and other primary commodities. In developed countries, where capital is relatively abundant and labour less so, it makes sense to focus on producing capital intensive goods.

In this way, all parties are assumed to derive benefit. The argument is that underdeveloped countries and developed countries will be absolutely better off if they specialise in this way and trade with each other. However, there are serious flaws in this theory, which undermine its expected outcome in practice. These flaws are no secret. The dominance of the theory of comparative advantage in dictating policy has not been due to the merit of its argument. Rather its appeal is because of its utility as a political tool. Therefore Theresa Hayter[47] has written, 'The theories of free trade and comparative advantage have held powerful sway in the West. They are propounded as a scientific explanation of reality, but they are, in fact, ideological tools.'

Ha-Joon Chang[48] has illustrated several of the flaws in the theory, as applied in reality. One is that the theory assumes that productive resources can move freely from one economic activity to another. In the case of labour, it assumes that a worker can immediately find employment in the new area of activity that comes to the fore when specialisation occurs. In the case of fixed capital, it assumes that, for example, a factory can be used immediately for a wholly new purpose once it is no longer required for its original purpose. This would be particularly important where tariff reductions bring about the collapse of an industry. Obviously, this assumption drastically oversimplifies reality. The evidence points to the contrary. Whole swathes of Mexican industry, which had been 'painstakingly built up' behind protective walls, were wiped out as the country liberalised in the 1980s and 1990s.[49] The workforce in Mexico did not automatically find new employment, as the theory would predict, and the result was a slow-down in economic growth and widespread job losses.

The theory of comparative advantage predicts that although there will be winners and losers from trade liberalisation, overall

47. 1990:50
48. 2007:71
49. Ibid

the gain to the winners will be greater than the loss to the losers.[50] This is termed the 'compensation principle', and predicts that the change to free trade is worth making since the winner can fully compensate the loser and still have something left. Chang cites the many examples of countries that introduced free trade, where economic growth has slowed or even reversed in the wake of such economic reform, as proof that the compensation principle does not apply in reality. Consideration must also be given to the importance of the role played by the welfare state in developed economies, in facilitating a limited compensation of those who lose out through trade liberalisation. The welfare state struggles to exist in most underdeveloped countries. Consequently the compensation principle can hardly apply to them. It's reasonable, therefore, to conclude that trade liberalisation can wreck livelihoods. This can often be a matter of life and death in poor countries with no social safety net.[51]

The example of Kenyan trade liberalisation shows the damage that it can do. Kenya, along with all African countries, was forced to dismantle its tariff barriers in the 1980s, as a condition of winning approval for aid flows from the IMF.[52] The country reduced restrictions on imported clothing and deregulated the cotton market. Cheap European and Asian clothing flooded the market. In 1984, Kenya produced 70,000 bales of cotton. By 1995, it was only producing 20,000. In the late 1980s the industry employed around 320,000 people. By the late 1990s it only employed 220,000. By the end of the 1990s cotton production in Kenya was worth less than 5% of its value in the 1980s.[53] World prices for cotton fell by 50% in the 1990s, generating an estimated foreign exchange loss of $300 million for Sub Saharan African countries as a whole. This was brought about by heavily subsidised US cotton and the promotion of competitive exports throughout the Global South.[54]

The promotion of export dependence by the IFIs has led to the collapse of many industries and millions of livelihoods through-

50. Ibid, 72
51. Ibid
52. Glennie, 2008:39
53. Ibid
54. Ibid

out the Global South. One of the reasons for this, as evidenced in the previous example of world prices for cotton, results from a problem known as the 'fallacy of composition'. This problem is simply that when many countries are forced to rely on exporting primary commodities onto world markets, chronic oversupply will occur. Basic laws of supply and demand determine that prices will, therefore, collapse.[55] The reduction in the price for the commodities has many knock-on effects – workers being paid extremely poor wages, huge increases in the level of poverty and reduction in tax revenues leading to less spending on social services.

Prices for non-oil commodity declined by around one half in the 1980s and 1990s alone.[56] Many Least Developed Countries (LDCs) are dependent on exporting a small range of agricultural commodities and have therefore been particularly badly affected by this. Oversupply onto world markets has caused the prices for cocoa, coffee, rice, wheat, maize and a host of other commodities that poor countries depend on, to collapse. For example, the real price of cocoa fell by 6.9% per year from 1977 to 2001.[57]

The collapse in commodity prices has been accompanied by a collapse in the terms of trade for poor countries. Terms of trade represent the quantity of a country's imports that can be purchased with the proceeds of a given quantity of their exports. The 'Prebisch-Singer' hypothesis has been shown to predict that the long term relative price for internationally traded commodities will decline relative to that for manufactures.[58] This hypothesis is based on the observation that the relative price-elasticity of demand for commodities is less than that for manufactures. Simply put, there is a limited demand for commodities such as rice on global markets. New manufactured products, on the other hand, constantly generate new demand. Consequently, the internationally traded price of these, relative to commodities, tends to rise over time. The result of this is that underdeveloped countries must export more and more commodities over time to pay for the same

55. Lines, 2008:39
56. Buckland, 2004:67
57. Ibid
58. Todaro and Smith, 2003:522-525

quantity of manufactured imports. This results in acceleration in natural resources and commodities out of the country, while the flow of goods into the country reduces with time. In short, there is a real net flow of wealth out of the Global South into the Global North.

The dollar price of internationally traded commodities fell by 31% between 1977 and 2005, when set against the prices of manufactured goods that underdeveloped countries import.[59] Between 1981/82 and 2001/03, the terms of trade for LDCs fell by 35%. At the end of this period, a given amount of their exports could pay for around a third less of imports, than at the beginning.[60] This has facilitated the ongoing and increasing transfer of wealth from the developing to the developed countries. It has also caused the collapse of rural livelihoods throughout the developing world.

There are several other reasons why commodity prices have fallen continuously since the 1970s. One is that subsidies provided to agriculture by developed countries (Europe and the US in particular), often result in prices that are lower than the cost of production. Subsidised agricultural produce, often in the form of food aid, has flooded, or been 'dumped' on underdeveloped countries' economies, undermining local production.[61] The WTO has greatly facilitated developed countries in continuing to subsidise their agricultural sectors, while forcing underdeveloped countries to liberalise theirs.

Another reason is the increasing dominance of a small number of buyers for many commodities in the world market. This represents a concentration of purchasing power. In the US, the grocery sector entities controlled a little over 25% of all purchasing in 1992, and over 40% by 2000.[62] Similarly, the median market share of the five largest grocery producers in European states was over 80% in 2000. Dominance in purchasing has enabled these corporations to set prices for global agricultural commodities. In

59. Buckland, 2004:41
60. Ibid, 43
61. as in the case of Kenya in the above example and food aid in chapter 6
62. Kaplinsky, 2005:170-178

this way they have had the ability to drive them down. Low prices in stores are good for business, but the savings that customers make are not taken out of the store's profits. They extracted from the producers, leading to even higher levels of poverty.

Faced with declining terms of trade for their exports, many poor countries have devoted more and more land to export cash cropping. This is an attempt to earn sufficient foreign exchange to service their debts and pay for imports. Lines describes this as the poorest countries being forced, 'to run ever faster in order to stay where they are'.[63] The diversion of land to export cash cropping undermines food production for domestic needs. This generates one of two results: the need for greater food imports, or increased malnutrition and food shortages. Many poor rural people in developing countries, who are net purchasers of food, have found that the prices they pay for food have increased. This is because domestic food production has been undermined by export orientation. This is a cruel irony.

Of course, for developed countries, the decline in terms of trade for underdeveloped regions and their commodity exports has enhanced their trading position. Developed countries are guaranteed a flow of cheap commodities from export orientation policies in the South. The income from a given amount of developed country manufactured exports can purchase more imports of commodities from poor countries than was the case before. The availability of markets for the surplus generated by the subsidised agriculture in Europe and the US is another major boon for developed countries. The situation today seems not dissimilar to that of the colonial era.[64]

The WTO: TRIPs, TRIMs and the poor

Threats to withdraw aid have played a role in negotiations at the WTO. Beyond these mechanisms, there are other ways that WTO agreements have harmed the poor in underdeveloped countries.

One of the damaging WTO agreements is the Trade Related Aspects of Intellectual Property Rights (TRIPs) agreement. TRIPs

---

63. 2008:43
64. as discussed in chapter 5

emerged from the Uruguay round of the WTO negotiations in 1994.[65] The agreement requires members of the WTO to protect Intellectual Property Rights (IPRs). The main outcome of this is that MNCs have been able to enforce patents that they own. This prevents poor countries from developing generic alternatives to new technologies. IPRs have been enforced in areas as diverse as seeds (for example US MNCs have developed and patented new strains of Basmati rice and Mexican beans), and anti-retroviral medicines for use in treating HIV.

The enforcement of IPRs has increased the flow of rents from the developing to the developed countries. Rent refers to the super-normal profits that MNCs can obtain through having a monopoly control of these technologies. Since the agreement prohibits poor countries from producing generic alternatives to patented technologies, developing countries are forced to purchase these from Northern MNCs. This results in a flow of tribute from South to North. In 2000, this was expected to cost Mexico and Brazil $526 million and $1.7 billion in rent transfers to Northern MNCs. As Buckland writes, 'These expenditures, particularly when they push wealth from the South to the North, also create lost opportunities in areas of more basic human needs, like food, sanitation and health.'[66]

A major negative effect of TRIPs has been to deny countries that face a HIV/AIDs epidemic access to essential medicines, since the patents on anti-retrovirals are protected under the agreement. Consequently, only 3 million of the 9.7 million people in need of anti-retrovirals in poor countries received them in 2007.[67] The HIV/AIDs pandemic is more than a public health emergency in its own right. In Sub-Saharan Africa the level of sickness and mortality it has inflicted on the working age population is so high, that the disease has become a major impediment to economic growth and contributed greatly to increased poverty. In 2007, up to 5 million people in Sub-Saharan Africa who needed anti-retrovirals had no access to them.[68] Many of the more effect-

65. Buckland, 2004:121-128
66. Buckland, 2004:125
67. UNDP, 2008:30

ive anti-retrovirals are prohibitively expensive, even for patients and health authorities in the developing world. For many in the Global South there will never be any possibility that they will be able to afford the drugs.

In agriculture, the patenting of seeds is facilitating to MNCs in extracting rents from poor farmers in poor countries. This has been achieved through the protection/patenting of what are termed 'plant breeder's rights'. Prior to the patenting of new seed varieties, peasants would typically reserve their own seeds for the following year, from the current year's harvest. However, with MNCs patenting new seeds (74% of new biotechnology patents granted in the US by 1998 had been given to a small number of MNCs) the face of global agriculture is changing.[69]

New 'terminator' seeds, patented by MNCs, produce plants that grow sterile seed. Farmers are therefore locked in a system where they have to purchase new, patented seeds, every year.[70] These seeds could, even when farmers reject their use, infect traditional crop, and result in a portion of their seed becoming sterile.[71] This is a worrying development. The WTO has also attempted to enforce patents of a host of new varieties of seeds. A study was conducted in Argentina, Uruguay and Chile to assess this new form of patenting in agricultural inputs. Unsurprisingly it found that this had increased the power of plant breeders (MNCs), and increased the power of seed suppliers (MNCs) in the agricultural sector. This process threatens to result in a massive flow of wealth from peasants in the South, to MNCs in the North.[72]

Overall, the combination of free trade rules and IPRs has enabled a new industrialised global agriculture to emerge. In this new arrangement, MNCs control the entire agricultural production chain. Since the seeds are becoming commoditised, and MNCs own the rights to them, they are increasingly commodifying the input market. This facilitates the domination of the input side of

68. Ibid
69. Buckland, 2004
70. Bello, 2009:33
71. Madeley, 1999:33
72. Buckland, 2004:128

the production chain. But domination is also occurring in the production arena. Big input producers who sell seeds and fertilisers
together with big farmers and big retailers become vertically
integrated in production chains. This new system of agricultural
production is squeezing out small-holder peasants, as they are
forced from their land to make way for large scale and monopolistic
farming practices.

In 1994 WTO made an agreement referred to as the Trade
Related Investment Measures (TRIMs) agreement. This agreement prevents countries in which MNCs invest from requiring
them to use local labour and materials.[73] Local producers, who
could link into their production processes by providing some of
their inputs, are often prevented from doing this, since MNCs are
not obliged to source inputs in the countries in which they operate. The resulting lack of linkages that emerges, between MNCs
and the countries in which they operate, enables them to easily
move location internationally, if cost savings can be made in
another country. The possibility of fostering sustainable economic
growth through foreign direct investment by MNCs is therefore
denied to poor countries.

Since MNCs are freed up by this agreement to move location
easily, they have been able to play the workforces of different
countries off against each other. Consequently the employment
that they generate is more precarious and low paid than it would
be in the absence of TRIMs. When MNCs can easily source their
materials and labour in another lower cost location, they induce a
'race to the bottom' as underdeveloped countries endeavour to
attract and retain their investment. Countries that have laws in
place to protect labour rights or a minimum wage, will find that
MNCs can very easily decide to locate elsewhere.[74]

These WTO agreements have all harmed poor people in the
developing world, albeit in different ways. For as long as many
poor countries are heavily dependent on aid, they will have a very
weak bargaining position in relation to the interests of rich countries, at the WTO. These agreements have, therefore, benefited

73. Madelely, 1999:10-11
74. Ibid

rich countries generally, and MNCs and global finance in particular. Needless to say, the poor have not benefited.

Conclusion

The strength of the international financial and trade institutions, coupled with policies designed to protect the financial interest of the developed West, has serious negative consequences for the poorest countries. The global economic model extracts wealth from underdeveloped regions to the benefit of the wealthy interests and MNCs in the developed world. There is evidence that US direct investment abroad, including income from financial investments, was worth 30% of domestic profits in 1970. This income raced up to being worth 100% cent of domestic profits by 2000.[75] This clearly evidences a substantial flow of wealth from the South to the North.

The degree to which the pursuit of free, liberalised trade and economics have enabled wealthy interests in the west to profit at the expense of the developing world is astounding. David Harvey posits that neoliberal economics has, from the outset, been a deliberate political project by the global capitalist elite (primarily based in the US, Japan and Europe) to consolidate their power as a class, through bolstering the power of financial capital throughout the world.[76] It is therefore no surprise that economic globalisation has enriched the few and impoverished the many, since it has entailed the extension of imperialism into a new era of financial dominance. Aid, far from promoting the well-being of the poor in the Third World, has been used to facilitate the transition to this new era.

This new group of powerful financial interests effectively draws from the lifeblood of the developing world. Its reach is extensive, impacting on every aspect of the lives of the world's poorest people. Human life has become a manipulated commodity. The interests of finance can hold an entire country to ransom with the full moral backing of international law. Every day more and more of the world's most impoverished people are being lost to

75. Dumenil and Levy
76. Harvey 2005

the shadowy world of the critically poor. Compassion and human dignity come second to financial gain.

CHAPTER SEVEN

The Macroeconomic Effects of Aid

Large volumes of aid can have a significant impact on the value of recipient countries' exchange rates. They create currency appreciation, through an effect known as 'Dutch Disease' that undermines key aspects of the recipients' economies. It is important to understand these impacts since large volumes of ODA are required by the Millennium Project to achieve its goals (MDGs). These large financial flows are required to kick start capital accumulation, and hence investment, in poor countries. It is from this process that the poor are expected to benefit as the effects of economic growth 'trickle down' to them. This 'reality' has been carefully scripted by the powerful in the Global North for public consumption. It is this message that has been supported enthusiastically by politicians, celebrities, the media and many NGOs. That so many people with a genuine passion for poverty eradication across the planet have been drawn to this falsehood is testament to the appeal of the deception. ODA as a cure for all the world's poverty ills will continue to be championed by the unwitting, the well-meaning, and the real beneficiaries.

The reasoning ought to be challenged. The reality is that capital accumulation in poor countries is undermined primarily by massive ongoing externalisation of resources from their economies.[1] ODA has contributed to precisely the scenario that has retarded growth in underdeveloped countries. There is no conclusive evidence that flows of aid are related to economic growth in aid recipient countries. Rather, global economic growth and economic growth in underdeveloped countries have tended to benefit the poor little, if at all.

Currency Appreciation – Dutch Disease
In the 1960s, natural gas revenues flooded into the Netherlands.

1. For the reasons already put forward in this book.

The economy was suddenly hit with a large amount of foreign currency seeking to buy up the exported gas. The gas had to be paid for in the domestic currency. There was, obviously, only a limited supply of domestic currency for which it could be exchanged. This led to a steep rise in the value of the domestic currency. The currency appreciation choked off the export sector, as the price of exports rose, and led to increasing unemployment.[2]

It has since been recognised that large inflows of foreign exchange, in the form of ODA, to underdeveloped countries, can have a similar effect. In this situation a limited supply of the domestic currency must 'mop up' a much larger supply of foreign currency. This is because the foreign currency cannot be spent directly in the recipient economy. It must be exchanged for the domestic currency in order to be spent. The result is an appreciation in the domestic currency's value that consequently makes the aid recipient's exports more expensive. Rising export sector unemployment can then be a severe problem in poor countries, especially those which rely on exporting commodities.[3] In Ethiopia, it has been estimated that future scaling up of aid could lead to currency appreciation of 20%.[4] This, it has been estimated, could lead to exports falling from 14% of GDP to just 8% of GDP, by 2015. If this scenario were to come about, the effects on wages and employment in the export sector would be severe. Because there will be fewer exports and less tax revenues being generated, there will be an overall negative effect on the country's wealth. This will lead to higher levels of poverty and an increased need for ODA, with a fresh set of accompanying poverty-inducing conditions.

Although this book has been critical of the IMF's approach of tackling inflation at all costs, it must be acknowledged that inflation can harm the poor, especially when the value of their cash income declines. When the exchange rate is fixed rather than floating, currency fluctuations obviously cannot happen, but rising inflation can be a common occurrence. Governments then find

2. Moyo, 2009:62-65
3. Ibid
4. Glennie 2008:85

that they are forced to raise interest rates to combat this inflation. This action undermines economic growth and employment.[5] Tanzania suffered inflation in 1999, due to large inflows of foreign aid. This led to credit being controlled more tightly, and hampered the expansion of firms in the country.[6]

There are various methods available to recipient countries to control the negative effects of currency appreciation but these are not without cost. Governments can, for example, issue local-country debt in order to 'soak up' some of the foreign exchange. The cost of this is the interest incurred by the government. In Uganda, in 2005, the government issued $700 million in aid-related bonds, incurring an interest cost to the tax payer of $110 million.[7] When aid is provided as loans, this type of interest payment is in addition to the interest that the government pays on the original loan. Obviously, this creates a double burden for the tax payer. If foreign currency received as aid is spent on imports, the currency appreciation effects are negated, which can be advantageous for food-importing countries. However, cheap food imports can out-compete domestic food production, harming the agricultural sector. Dutch Disease is a complicated problem that is not easily mitigated by underdeveloped countries that receive large amounts of aid.

Economic Growth as the key to Poverty Reduction
A key claim made by advocates of aid, in the context of the commitment among donors to achieve the Millennium Development Goals (MDGs) by 2015, is that aid promotes economic growth. This, in turn, it is argued, will bring about a reduction in poverty in the developing world. A key advisor to The UN Millennium Project put forward this argument: 'Long-term poverty reduction requires sustained economic growth, which in turn depends on technological advance and capital accumulation.'[8] The report goes on to say that capital accumulation requires investment, which can come from private household savings, public investments drawn

---

5. Glennie 2008:84
6. Ibid
7. Moyo, 2009: 65
8. UN 2005:28

from government revenue, savings from abroad, foreign assistance or borrowing. The report warns that, 'When the process of capital accumulation breaks down, economic growth and poverty reduction break down.'[9]

The report provides the orthodox explanation for why economic development has failed in the poorest countries. It argues that severe resource constraints become a common problem that results in a 'poverty trap' for poor countries. In this trap, the process of capital accumulation breaks down. The report sees this resource constraint as typified by a range of factors. Among other factors are low savings rates. In this scenario, the poor must spend their income and cannot save. Another factor is low tax revenue. This results in governments lacking the necessary resources to make essential public investments in human capital (e.g. health, education) and infrastructure. Yet another factor is low foreign investment, often as a result of a lack of infrastructure in the country in question.[10] The report goes on to state that:

> The poorest countries save too little to achieve economic growth, and aid is too low to compensate for the low domestic savings rate ... The result of low saving rates – unless offset by foreign assistance [ODA] or foreign investments [which are not about the transpire for the aforementioned reasons] – is a chronic decline in capital per person and a consequent chronic decline in income *per capita*.[11]

This reasoning forms the logical basis for the renewed calls for increases in ODA to meet the MDGs. Aid, it is believed, can substitute for a low domestic savings rate in poor countries. It will also, according to this thinking, provide the necessary investment to kick start capital accumulation. This, it is hoped, will lead to economic growth, rising incomes of the poor; and ultimately a 'virtuous circle' of increasing domestic savings followed by further investment, economic growth and poverty reduction. An attempt to quantify the amount of ODA required to meet the

9. Ibid, 29
10. Ibid, 35
11. Ibid, 38-39

MDGs is made in the report. The estimate suggests that 2002 ODA levels will need to rise by 87% by 2010. A further rise to 130% on 2002 levels will be required between 2010 and 2015 (to $195 billion in that year), to meet the goals.[12]

It should be apparent to the reader that this account of the role that aid can play in a poor country is severely at odds with the typology of aid presented in this book. In light of what we have learned in preceding chapters about the role that aid has played, this chapter offers an alternative view to this account of aid's role. It is important to recall that aid has played a large part in structuring the world economy in such a way that the Global North has been able to perpetuate a system that extracts wealth from the Global South. This is does for the benefit of elitist interests.

Yash Tandon analyses the reasons why domestic savings rates are low in poor countries. He notes that 'external expenditure' (money leaving the country) is a major drag on the domestic savings rate. He offers the following explanations for low domestic savings:

Domestic expenditure is high because the rich spend huge amounts on imported luxuries that do not benefit the domestic economy. This results from the extreme inequality in poor countries.

Domestic savings are reduced by corrupt officials externalising misappropriated wealth into foreign tax havens. He notes that 'project fees' paid to corrupt officials are typically 10% and are often paid into foreign bank accounts.

Domestic savings are reduced by Multi National Corporations (MNCs) being able to export profits with ease (often through transfer pricing: over-pricing imports and under-pricing exports that take place within the global operation of the firm, so that their accounts do not display profits from value-added in a particular country. MNCs frequently avoid paying taxes in countries that attempt to apply taxation to them in this way and instead launder these profits through tax havens such as Ireland). Christian Aid (2008) estimates that commercial tax evasion represents an outflow of funds from underdeveloped countries of $325 to $520 billion per year.

---

12. Ibid, 251

Domestic savings are reduced by payments made to corrupt politicians/bureaucrats into foreign bank accounts.

Worsening terms of trade (resulting from the export orientation imposed as a condition of aid – see chapter 6) leads to a worsening balance of payments, reducing domestic savings.

Speculation in financial markets leads to capital flight, which reduces domestic savings. High levels of external debt servicing also reduces domestic savings. Much of this debt is 'odious', meaning that it was misappropriated when it was received (in many cases illegally), and therefore, in all likelihood, failed to contribute to domestic savings at any time and had no beneficial outcome for poor people when it was incurred.

War makes domestic expenditure high (reducing savings). Wars in underdeveloped countries have fuelled (and been fuelled by) the massive profits that the Northern arms industry has made through sales of weapons to underdeveloped countries.[13]

All of this adds up to a massive flow of resources out of underdeveloped countries and into developed countries of the Global North. It is estimated that this outward flow of resources from poor countries is happening faster now than during colonial times.[14] It is clear that rather than trying to plug the savings gap with ODA, the focus should be on trying to reverse this outflow of resources. ODA has contributed in a large measure to creating this situation. Offering ODA as the solution is therefore counter to any logical reasoning.

Many of the policies that have promoted this externalisation of funds from poor countries have been promoted through conditions attached to aid. ODA has also undermined democratic accountability in many poor countries and promoted corruption and clientalism. This has promoted the flow of finance from poor countries to foreign tax havens. Christian Aid[15] has estimated that illicit outflows of finance from underdeveloped countries amount to $500 to $800 billion per year, with commercial tax evasion representing 65% of this amount. Globally, tax evasion

13. Adapted from Tandon, 2008:93-94
14. Ibid, 94
15. Christian Aid 2008

alone represents a far greater outflow of resources from poor coun-tries than ODA represents in inflows. Even if we ignore the fact that ODA has contributed to the creation of this situation, the gap between these outflows and inflows of ODA is so large, that ODA could never compensate for the difference. The era of 'aid optimism' was supposed to be one in which the outward flow was stemmed, while the inward flow increased. Over time the gap between the haves in the Global North and the have-nots in the Global South would be reduced, and eventually a fair equilibrium would be established. It is quite clear that such equilibrium can never be attained using the policies employed. One must ask if this is much to the relief, and to the continued benefit, of powerful interest groups.

Aid and Economic Growth

There is a question that has perplexed academics for a long time: Do flows of ODA lead to economic growth? There exists a huge range of literature arguing, or indeed purporting to 'prove' that it does, and likewise a huge range of literature purporting to 'prove' that it does not. Economists typically employ regression type analyses to attempt to assert an answer, one way or the other. Regression is a statistical method that involves attempting to observe if a movement in a dependant variable (in this case rates of economic growth) is related to (or correlates with) a movement in an independent variable (in this case provision of ODA), across a sample of data large enough to accurately represent the whole. The independent variable is considered to be the 'cause' and the dependent variable is considered to be the 'effect', or outcome, of the change in the independent variable. In conducting these analyses, economists often attempt to 'control' for the existence of other factors that could influence economic growth. In this way they attempt to determine whether ODA does or does not have an effect on economic growth independently of these other influencing fac-tors.[16] Some analyses seek to discover if aid, in tandem with some other influence (such as the policy environment in the recipient

---

16. Some of these other influencing factors might be the existence of armed conflict, regime type, the existence of large scale natural resource extraction industries etc.

country) has an influence on growth, and attempt to control for other influences. Economists seek 'statistically significant' results when they conduct these analyses. 'Statistically significant' means results that are very unlikely to be chance occurrences.

More simply put, it is almost like stating that global warming is directly related to the amount of household waste being sent to landfill. In investigating this link the control of, or measures to take into account other factors that might cause global warming, are completely ignored – emissions from factories; car emissions; volcanic activity, or any of the other factors widely believed to contribute to global warming. To try to establish any link between the levels of waste going to landfill and global warming under these conditions would be so tenuous as to be meaningless.

The problem with these regressions, when applied to aid and growth, is that economies are very complex systems, which cannot easily be analysed in terms of just a few variables. There are a huge range of factors that may or may not effect economic growth or contraction in an individual economy. It is impossible to control for all of these. Geography, climate, domestic and international politics, markets for commodities and manufactures, trade deals, tariffs, migration within and between countries, public health and foreign investment are just a few of the factors that contribute in different ways to aggregate economic growth rates. Even when a statistical relationship has been established between dependent and independent variables and includes controlling variables, the issue of causality is not certain.

Singling out the effect of ODA on economic growth and 'proving' an effect one way or the other should rightly be seen as a virtually impossible task: perhaps even an abuse of a statistical method. Howard White has highlighted,

> these conclusions [regarding the relationship of aid to growth] are founded upon cross-country regressions, which have numerous weaknesses when applied to the aid-growth relationship. These shortcomings mean that such approaches cannot be used to decide whether aid works or not, and certainly not to inform more intricate aspects of aid policy and management.[17]

17. White, 2009:211

In reality, the supposedly 'proven' relationship of aid to economic growth has not merely been used to justify 'intricate' aspects of aid policy and management, but rather has been used to legitimise the greatest global scaling up of ODA that has ever occurred. This should be a cause of major concern to the aid optimists.

Such is the degree of confusion and disagreement within the aid/growth literature, that in one edited volume entitled *Development Aid: A Fresh Look*,[18] the editor's introduction states confidently that:

> The late 1990s saw a fundamental change in the literature on aid and growth ... they use better cross-country empirical data ... are based on more informative theories about the determinants of growth, and use better data. These studies provide a reasonably clear and consistent message that growth could on average be lower in the absence of aid [a statistically significant result].[19]

The authors include reference to the article that they (and many others) describe as 'seminal' within this supposed consensus on the success of aid at promoting growth: Burnside and Dollar (1997), 'Aid, Policies and Growth'. It should be noted that this article was published by the World Bank, an institution with a very strong interest in obtaining just the sort of results that this paper reported. Its findings have been widely refuted.

However, in the very same volume, the carpet is swept from under this cosy consensus. Picciotto's contribution[20] draws attention to the reality that the variability in growth between countries is not obviously related to levels of aid. There are countries, like Korea, that receive large amounts of aid and achieve rapid economic growth. Less successfully, there are countries, like Ethiopia and Zambia, that receive vast amounts of aid but achieving no *per capita* income growth. Worse still Malawi, Niger and Honduras received large amounts of aid in 2001 yet experiencing negative

18. Mavrotas and McGillivray eds, 2009
19. Ibid 2009:3
20. Picciotto 2009:183

per capita income growth. Finally, there are countries, most notably China and Angola that receive little aid,[21] yet they still achieve rapid economic growth. Such variance in countries' experiences questions the solidity of any claim about a general association of aid to growth.

A further contribution in the same volume reports that:

> Much analysis of aid impact has been at the macro level, and much of it has lent support to the aid pessimists by finding a slight link, or none at all, between aid and growth. But, in contrast, others say that the evidence points to a clear impact of aid on growth (for example, in the first chapter of this volume). The literature appears so inconclusive that there is not even a consensus on whether there is a consensus![22]

At this point it should be obvious that it is easy for any writer to draw conclusions about the relationship of aid to growth. All that is required is that the writer draws on previously published material that fits with his or her own perspective. Such are the weaknesses and unreliability inherent in the published research, the safest, and most honest conclusion is to observe that any clear relationship between ODA and economic growth is, perhaps, unknowable. The thesis of this work is that aid has not contributed significantly to economic growth in poor countries. There is certainly no strong evidence to refute this claim in the aid / growth literature, given the weaknesses in the methodologies employed.

Economic Growth and Poverty Reduction

There is little to give confidence that aid does indeed lead to economic growth in poor countries. But, put that concern aside for the moment. Then assume that, somehow, it does. Attention can then be turned to assessing whether economic growth is actually capable of contributing to poverty reduction. In particular, there is a need to assess if economic growth is capable of achieving sufficient poverty reduction to meet the first MDG target: to reduce, between 1990 and 2015, the proportion of the global population living on

---

21. i.e. aid to GNP of less than 3 per cent
22. White, 2009:211

under $1 a day by half. The UNDP and World Bank estimate of the percentage of the World's population living on under $1 a day was 29% in 1990 and 18% in 2004.[23] However, it is important to recall that there is a great deal of controversy surrounding how best to measure extreme poverty.[24] These estimates could be dramatically undercounting the number of extremely poor in the world.

By whatever estimate is chosen, future economic growth will need to contribute significantly to poverty reduction if this particular MDG is to be achieved. However, as this book has argued, the policies pursued, and promoted through ODA, over the last 30 years have not been in the interests of the poor. This has implications for the effect that economic growth has on poverty reduction. It is important to remember that the type of economic growth that has been promoted is part of the neoliberal agenda.

Economic growth along neoliberal lines often dramatically increases inequality. This can make the poor not only relatively, but absolutely worse off due to the effect that inequality has on rising inflation.[25] There is also evidence that economic growth can occur in a country without having any impact on poverty reduction. Under Structural Adjustment Policies, economic growth in Tanzania proceeded at 4% per year from 1990 to 2000, but the proportion of people living under the poverty line fell only slightly. When population growth in Tanzania of 3% per annum is accounted for, the statistics show that the total number of poor people in the country actually increased during the decade.[26]

It has been estimated that in middle income societies, such as Namibia, the Philippines and Ukraine, the poor share only 3.5% to 7.5% of the additional income achieved through economic growth.[27] In the poorest and most unequal societies, the poor receive very few of the benefits of growth. For example, in The Central African Republic 82.5% of the population lives below the $2 a day poverty line. The 17.5% of people above this poverty line

23. UNDP, 2007:24
24. See Chapter 2
25. Glennie, 2008:80
26. Glennie, 2008:78
27. Woodward and Simms, 2006:10

receive 76% of the benefits of increased income due to economic growth in the country.[28]

Throughout the period 1981 to 2001, global GDP increased by $18,691 billion.[29] Of this amount, only $278 billion was received by those under the $1 a day poverty line, just 1.5% of the total. As global markets and economies became more deregulated and liberalised in the 1990s, the poverty reduction effect of economic growth fell sharply. In the 1980s, $151 billion of the total increase in global GDP, representing 2% of the total increase, was received by those under the $1 a day poverty line. Low though this figure was, it fell even further in the 1990s. In the 1990s, just $95 billion of the total increase in global GDP was received by those under the $1 a day poverty line. This represents just 0.8% of the total increase in global GDP. From these statistics, we can see that as economic globalisation proceeded through the 1980s and 1990s, the benefit to the world's poor of economic growth fell sharply both in absolute and relative terms.

When adjusted for population growth, in the 1990s it took $166 of global economic growth to contribute just $1 to poverty reduction.[30] Redistribution of just 0.12% of the income of the richest 1% of the world's population would have had the same effect on poverty reduction as all the growth in global GDP during that time.[31] Given this reality, it is clear that economic growth, of the type that has been pursued since the early 1980s, and which has been promoted through ODA, will not bring about the promised outcome of halving the proportion of the world's poor. However, it is evident that the real beneficiaries of economic growth are the rich. They are keen to maintain the illusion that economic growth will bring about a transformation for the better in the circumstances of the poor in coming years. This is a baseless myth.

Conclusion
It is evident that ODA can have a serious and negative effect on

28. Ibid
29. Woodward and Simms, 2006:13
30. Ibid, 15
31. Ibid

the value of a recipient country's exchange rate, through the phenomenon known as Dutch Disease. While it may be possible to mitigate some of these negative effects, attempts to do this are not without negative macroeconomic consequences. The generally held consensus is that aid contributes to economic growth and hence poverty reduction. However, when every part of this supposed causal chain is examined, the consensus is found to be without merit. Specifically, the immediate reason for poor countries' continued poverty may be a lack of domestic savings and hence capital accumulation and investment. This, generally, has occurred in the context of massive outflows of resources from the Global South to the Global North.

Given this scenario, it is absurd to propose that ODA should be used to bridge this savings gap in poor countries in order to promote growth and achieve the MDGs. First of all, aid has promoted the development of this scenario. It can only be assumed, therefore, that more aid would further structure the relationship between the Global North and the Global South along these lines. Secondly, ODA inflows will never match the rate of expropriation of wealth from the Global South by the Global North. If this was to occur, much of the rationale for providing ODA would be lost for donors, since their self interest would no longer be served. A radical new approach is needed that focuses on stopping the rapid externalisation of resources from developing countries.

There is no consensus in the academic literature concerning the role that aid, in the form of ODA, can play in promoting economic growth. The arguments put forward in this book suggest that aid can, in fact, often undermine economic growth in poor countries. The aid/growth literature, contrary to common perception, allows for this possibility. The evidence suggests that the economic growth pursued has benefited the poor less and less as these policies have become increasingly dominant from the 1980s to the present.

It is tempting to despair that any improvement is possible in the lives of the poor in the underdeveloped world. Given the degree of inequality and the power imbalances that exist in the world, there may be little reason for optimism. However, it is possible to conceive alternatives from which social justice on a global level could be forged. This requires radical thinking, especially in terms of global power relationships. However, it is not impossible for this to come about. All those who seek social justice in the world today should speak out against the crippling 'strait-jacket' that ODA has imposed on the underdeveloped world. This begins with advocating for meaningful change in the relationships between the rich and poor. The following chapter offers recommendations toward such meaningful change.

CHAPTER EIGHT

Recommendations for Meaningful Change

It would be wrong to suggest that all aid is bad. Aid can and has delivered some very significant results. The G8 summit in Gleneagles may, as Bob Geldof acknowledged 'fall far short of what many wanted' but the measures agreed on Africa would save 10 million lives.[1] This book is not a criticism of aid in all circumstances. That would be to ignore major contributions to the alleviation of suffering. No one can dispute the value and impact of The Expanded Programme of Immunisation. Launched in 1974, this programme can boast success in increasing the rate of vaccination against six key diseases from 5% of children, to 75% of children by 1990.[2] In practical, day-to-day terms the impact of this programme continues, saving an estimated 3 million lives a year, and preventing a further 750,000 children a year from becoming permanently disabled. This, and a host of other targeted initiatives have delivered achievements that are to be celebrated. Targeting, with defined objectives, it has been evidenced, creates the greatest potential for success.[3] It is a tragedy, therefore, that much overseas aid is not given, or lent, for purposes that have such a direct, targeted objective. When aid is seen and used as the driver of economic growth, the game plan is that the poor will benefit indirectly from the 'trickle down effect'. 'Trickle down' is purely aspirational, lacking the specific targets and objectives necessary to maximise the potential for success. Interestingly, a hierarchy of beneficiaries is established even in the very title 'trickle down', the poor being the lowest! The new 'aid optimism' that defined the opening years of the 21st century relied heavily

---

1. http://news.bbc.co.uk/2/hi/business/4666743.stm *and*
http://news.bbc.co.uk/2/hi/business/4663659.stm
2. Glennie 2008:28
3. Ibid

on and was driven by the questionable paradigm of aid as the driver of economic growth. The UN Millennium Project Report in 2005, reiterated this rationale when it called for more aid.[4]

Despite great and laudable achievements, ODA is failing to alleviate poverty in the world today. In a very real sense ODA is contributing to the creation of poverty and maintaining inequality. This has results when donors impose self-serving policies as conditions attached to aid. Where this happens, donors and governments in recipient countries enter into clientalist relationships, which are mutually self-serving. The donors gain because they can create conditions that allow them to extract wealth from the Global South. Meanwhile, political elites in developing nations gain since ODA affords them the opportunity to avoid unpopular alternative means of revenue collection. In this way they can retain the loyalty of those whose support is essential for their continuance in power. In the midst of this are the poor, whose voices are rarely heard. Their interests are not served by the global aid regime. The reasonably minded reader is rightly outraged when the poor suffer through the misappropriation of ODA by corrupt elites. Perhaps more shockingly, but with less notice or comment, the poor have suffered greatly because of the economic policies imposed by donors. The poor constitute the group whose lives are most negatively impacted by the 'system' yet are most powerless to do anything to change the *status quo*.

Poverty has been accentuated by the economic policies enforced through aid conditions. These necessarily generate poverty in the South in order to generate wealth in the North. The poor suffer through declining terms of trade for agricultural and other commodities, brought about by policies focused on growth and liberalised markets. These policies result in dwindling incomes for peasant producers and collapsing rural livelihoods. Revenue collection in the country in which they live is undermined by the removal of import tariffs. Subsequently, food aid or subsidised food imports undermine the prices for the commodities that they produce. The poor suffer again when they lose access to essential services such as healthcare and education, because donors have

---

4. UN Millennium Project Report 2005

insisted that their government must slash spending to receive more aid. Once more, the poor feel the pressure when their access to electricity and water is curtailed as a result of privatisation, often imposed as one of the conditions on aid. Needless to say, this enriches Multi National Corporations (MNCs). The increase in cost of services under privatisation is simply too high for the poor to afford. MNCs are often able to export their profits at will, employ workers at exploitative wages and avoid taking responsibility for the pollution and environmental degradation that they create. Lax regulation again places a burden on the poor. When the IMF forces governments to control inflation at all costs, and balance the budget in times of financial crisis, the investments of wealthy creditors are protected. This protection takes precedence even if this results in widespread job losses and collapsing incomes for the poor. In a multitude of ways, economic policies and aid conditionalities forced on recipient countries accentuate poverty.

All of this must stop if the Millennium Development Goals (MDGs) are to have any chance of being met by 2015. Apart from the MDGs, all of this must stop if social justice is ever to be achieved on a global scale. As long as the power imbalances that exist in the world remain as extreme as they are today, there can be little optimism that things will change. What is required is that those who seek justice are motivated to advocate for change and to suggest alternatives.

Alternative policies and practices require belief in a number of key fundamentals: equality, genuine partnership, accountability between the North and the South, and genuine ownership of development policy by the poor. We have already seen that the PDAE included 56 commitments structured around five core principles: ownership, alignment, harmonisation, managing for results and mutual accountability.[5] However, as long as efforts like PDAE fail to address the linkages between poverty, ODA, global trade and aid conditionalities, such efforts will remain nothing more than a veneer hiding a fundamental problem: a problem that condemns countless millions to dehumanising suffering. The intention of those who supported the campaign at

5. Chapter 3

Gleneagles may have been honourable. However, the outwork-ing of decisions taken there has disadvantaged the poor. A real alternative is urgently required. In any new system, the focus ought to be on how ODA is affecting the lives of the poor, rather than the current mantra of *more aid good, less aid bad*.

Compensatory Finance is amongst the possible alternatives available. The core principle of compensatory finance is straight-forward. The finance represents a debt. The party paying the debt is obliged to the recipient, as a means of making good a past wrong, caused to the recipient by the debtor. Former colonies, now aid recipient countries, surely have a legitimate claim to receive compensatory finance from the former colonial powers and present imperial powers. Yash Tandon describes some of the legitimate bases for the payment of compensatory finance by Europe to the African/Caribbean/Pacific (ACP) countries:

> A built-in structural division of labour based on the ACP countries providing human beings in the form of commodities [as slave labour], super exploited wage labour, and grossly under-priced natural resources. These were needed for the industrialisation of Europe from the 17th to the 20th centuries.
>
> Imbalanced trade and a balance of payments deficit result-ing from Europe's comparative advantage in manufactured products, equipment, services (such as shipping, insurance and banking) and products secured under intellectual property rights, arising out of this historical division of labour.
>
> The ensuing liberation struggle (from the end of the First World War to the liberation of South Africa in 1994) at enor-mous cost, particularly to the people of Africa, from which they have not yet fully recovered.
>
> The Cotonou and previous agreements that cemented in place a colonial-type, structured asymmetrical relationship over production and trade.[6]

That there exists a legitimate claim by the countries of the Global South for compensatory finance from the countries of the Global North is in no doubt. After all, the inequality that exists

6. Tandon, 2008:37

today between the North and the South is entirely the result of a legacy of the imperialist era and its modern manifestations. It was, and continues to be, at the expense of the colonised that the colonisers developed. But how would Compensatory Finance differ from ODA?

Compensatory Finance is fundamentally different from ODA because the relationship of power between donor and recipient is reversed. If compensatory finance was to be paid by the North to the South, the North would be the debtor, and the South the creditor. Given this reversal, the poor people of the South, to whom the debt is owed, could set the terms under which it should be paid. Penalties and levies could be imposed for failure to meet the payment. Policy conditions could be agreed with the debtor countries for non payment of a portion of the debt. There could be no question of the North attaching conditions to the payment of compensatory finance. As payment could not be withheld by the North for failure to meet conditions, compensatory finance would result in a much less volatile flow of funds. Compensatory finance could easily be substituted for ODA in the short to medium term. This would ensure that aid dependent countries, that currently rely on inward flows of aid, would not have this essential income stream undermined. This plan is not completely flawless as there is always a risk that some of the compensation paid to the poor nations could be misappropriated by corrupt ruling elites in those countries. In that sense, it shares a risk with ODA.

Compensatory Finance is already on the global agenda, albeit in a slightly different arena. So also is its resistance by the powerful! Yash Tandon argues that financing to mitigate the negative effects of climate change in the South should be made under a compensatory financing arrangement. These negative effects have been caused by Northern industrialisation and displaced onto the countries of the South.[7] This principle has been recognised internationally in the UN Framework Convention on Climate Change.[8] This convention recognises that developed countries have a historical responsibility to compensate underdeveloped

7. Tandon, 2008:36
8. Ibid

countries for the damage they have inflicted on them, through climate change, during their period of industrialisation.[9] The principle is further reflected in treaty provisions of the Framework. The provisions oblige developed countries to provide new and additional financial flows and technology transfer to underdeveloped countries. The objective is to help mitigate the effects of climate change.[10]

To date, the developed countries have not lived up to their treaty responsibilities under this agreement. That shouldn't be a surprise! Furthermore, the attempts by donors to formalise the World Bank as the provider of this finance at the recent Copenhagen Climate Change Conference can be interpreted as a strategy to undermine these treaties and the principle of compensatory finance. The World Bank, in all likelihood would attach its usual conditions that pertain to the ODA it distributes on any such climate change compensatory finance. That would transform the very essence of this finance from that of compensation to the all too familiar instrument of Northern control. Based on the historical record as servant of the rich, there ought to be no place for the World Bank in this role.

Any attempt to transform development financing requires a radical restructuring of decision-making mechanisms. If poverty and suffering are, finally, to be dealt a fatal blow, then the poor themselves must be given a meaningful stake in economic policy making. The focus has to be taken off economic growth from which the poor benefit little, while the rich rapidly increase their wealth. The focus of national economic policy in underdeveloped countries ought instead to be placed on achieving economic growth that is rooted in raising the incomes of the poor. Such radical transformation would include social and environmental objectives.[11]

This can be achieved, but it requires a complete reversal of some core, present realities. Most notably, if it is to be achieved, underdeveloped countries will need to be allowed to protect

9. Ibid
10. Ibid
11. Woodward and Simms, 2006:17-18

infant industries through tariffs. These tariffs could provide an important and reliable source of revenue, as well as encouraging industrialisation. Import tariffs could also be placed on agricultural commodities that the poor depend on for their livelihoods. This would ensure that the prices that they receive are protected from subsidised imports. For their part, Northern countries ought to stop 'dumping' the surplus that they produce through agricultural subsidies on poor countries, in the guise of food aid. Investments could be made in encouraging the production of crops that the poor consume, resulting in the price effect of increased supply. Of course, there would also be income effects contributing to poverty alleviation, rather than promoting export led agricultural production for Multi National Agrifood Corporations.[12] The reality is that poor countries have been losing out for a long time on international commodity markets, and jeopardising their food security in the process.[13] The new strategy offers a real opportunity to address this. Polanyi[14] has described the new strategy as 're-embedding' the economy within society, rather than forcing society to serve the economy.

The new approach would ensure that food self sufficiency, or food sovereignty, would be prioritised above international trade in agricultural commodities. For many countries this would entail refocusing their markets, away from world markets and onto regional as well as domestic markets. Africa could, for example, refocus her international trade towards trade links in staple foods between her states. This could go some way to emulating the historical success of India and China in achieving national level food security. In this way the continent could be empowered to escape from its historical dependence on Northern countries.[15] China and India both pursued policies of food sovereignty in the latter part of the twentieth century, and managed to avoid famine as a result. Both countries also benefited from having large internal markets. They both achieved considerable development outcomes

---

12. Ibid, 18
13. Bello, 2009:145
14. in ibid
15. Lines, 2008:144-147

as a result. Domestic control of food supply and a lack of dependence on food imports have historically played an important role in allowing countries to develop. Ultimately the power relationships in the global food supply chain need to be addressed. Of course, this has implications for Multi National Food Corporations. International agreements would be required to govern the markets in which they operate.[16]

Alongside these measures, the state could lead investment into public service provision in underdeveloped countries, unhindered by donor demands to privatise essential services. Publicly funded healthcare and education could contribute to enhancing the opportunities for the poor to live the sort of lives that they have reason to value. Likewise, electricity, sanitation and water provision could be prioritised, without donor demands to privatise these. As a result of being publicly funded, these services could be targeted to make provision for rural communities and the poor, precisely those who are overlooked by private suppliers. The radical new approach would replace profit with people at its focal point.

If poor countries had meaningful input to policy, they could abolish tax havens, used by the rich and MNCs to siphon wealth from underdeveloped countries. Illicit outflows of finance from underdeveloped countries amount to somewhere between $500 and $800 billion per year.[17] This is a concrete change that development NGOs in the North should be advocating for now. The G20 recently indicated support for the abolition of tax havens. All those who campaign for social justice need to press these governments to make good on this and commit to it. It is no longer good enough, or even justified to simply call for more aid. If tax havens were closed the result would be a financial boom for underdeveloped countries that aid alone could never hope to match.

Northern countries could reallocate a portion of their ODA away from direct provision to underdeveloped countries, and assign it to research and development. This research and development ought to focus on technologies that are socially and environ-

16. Ibid
17. Christian Aid, 2008

mentally beneficial for underdeveloped countries. Obviously, this ought to include appropriate medical technology to ensure further progress toward the health-related MDGs. It is well known that relatively small investments in appropriate medical technology can have a large and positive impact on public health in underdeveloped countries. Countries of the Global South have been locked into buying expensive technology from the North. Apart from its expense, it is often inappropriate. This must change. The new alternative offers this possibility. Home grown technology will better serve the needs of the poor nations, and in the process, close off one more substantial flow of money out of the country.

Debt relief must be made a priority. Much of the debt that has been incurred by Southern countries is 'odious'. This means that the money borrowed was never used for the improvement of the lives of the poor, but was instead siphoned off by the rich into luxury consumption and foreign tax havens. These actions, obviously, benefit banks and the rich, but not the poor. Yet, the burden of repaying this debt has fallen squarely on the poor in under-developed countries, through the Structural Adjustment Policies described in this book. African debt grew from $6 billion in 1970 to $200 billion by the mid-1990s – more than the annual GDP of the continent![18] Although the World Bank and IMF organised Heavily Indebted Poor Countries (HIPC) initiative has resulted in limited debt relief for some countries, this debt relief has come with the usual donor conditionality.

Debt relief has enabled some HIPC countries to make school-ing free of charge to millions of children who previously received no schooling whatsoever. This is true in Zambia, Uganda and Malawi.[19] Zambia announced in 2006 that basic healthcare would be free as a result of debt relief.[20] This provides a powerful argu-ment in favour of further debt relief for the country. The IMF has estimated that HIPC countries have been able to increase anti-poverty spending from 6.4% of GDP to 7.9%, between 1999 and

18. Moss, 2007:153
19. Glennie: 2008:29
20. Moss, 2007:158

2003, as a result of debt relief.[21] These countries have made good use of the additional resources made available to them through debt relief, which provides a strong argument in favour of abolishing the debt of all HIPC countries. What is more, this debt relief should be made without conditions, since conditions harm the poor.

Currency speculation can have a strong negative impact on the economies of poor countries.[22] Several innovative ideas have been put forward to counter such speculative activity on the one hand, and foster innovative flows of development finance on the other. These are all varieties of the Tobin Tax, first proposed in 1973 by economist James Tobin. He intended that the tax would 'throw sand in the wheels' of the foreign exchange market, driving speculators out of the market. He believed speculators to be the reason for currency markets to behave irrationally. Ultimately, he saw them as the cause of many currency crises.[23]

Two varieties of the Tobin Tax ought to be implemented. The first form focuses on preventing currency speculators from betting on a devaluation of a currency. Since devaluations are often up to 40%, the tax must be large, in order to negate the profit, and should be imposed when a currency's exchange rate goes outside a predetermined range. This would promote the stability of poor countries' currencies and avoid the damaging effects of currency crises and IMF 'bailouts' on the poor. The rationale for this tax is provided by Spahn.[24] The motivation for speculators to purposefully, negatively influence the economies of poor countries could be eliminated through this new tax system. Therefore, many currency crises would be eliminated. Where a crisis did take place it would of a genuine nature, requiring a genuine international response.

The second form of Tobin Tax is put forward by Schmidt[25] who showed that it is perfectly possible and straightforward for a country to impose a levy on transactions of its own currency. A

21. Ibid
22. see chapter 6
23. Spratt, 2006:16
24. 1996, in Spratt, 2006
25. 2001, in Spratt, 2006

tax such as this, explicitly aimed at raising revenue for development finance, would provide reliable revenue streams for meeting development objectives. This would greatly contribute to meeting the MDGs. While underdeveloped countries could raise such a tax to fund their development, Spratt[26] has shown that it would also be very straightforward for any developed country to levy such a tax. Taxes raised in the developed world could then be set aside as finance to assist underdeveloped countries. Obviously, this could be used as part of the compensatory finance obligations of developed to underdeveloped countries. The advantage of this latter variety of Tobin Tax is that it does not depend on international agreement for its implementation. It could be levied by any country on its own currency, acting alone, or indeed by a group of countries acting in concert.

Southern countries are increasingly borrowing from each other or from the open market in order to avoid having to borrow from the World Bank, and accept its policy conditions.[27] The recent financial and economic crisis has exposed the perils of global financial and market integration: the bedrock of economic policies upon which growth strategies are built. The risks and disadvantages of integration in the global economy can now be seen to outweigh the few potential benefits for underdeveloped countries. These countries are now seeking alternatives to the policies that have brought about a worldwide recession, and from which many of them are suffering greatly. There are huge challenges for the World Bank because it relies on global financial markets, to raise the capital on which it operates. The undermining of these markets is creating a crisis, both of finance and legitimacy, for the World Bank. There has perhaps never been a better time for a radical re-think on the role and power of the World Bank. The time to act is now.

Perhaps the World Bank is hoping to get a new lease of life by becoming the conduit for climate change financing. That could represent investments of trillions rather than billions of dollars.[28]

26. Ibid
27. Tandon, 2008:120
28. Ibid

Any such development carries great risks for underdeveloped countries. The correct and appropriate channel for this financing is the UN Framework Convention on Climate Change, which already carries legally binding treaty commitments within its terms. The World Bank should be allowed to wind down its activities and eventually fade away, as underdeveloped countries achieve development on their own terms.

The IMF has been involved in 'mission creep' since 1971, the year in which the gold standard was abolished. It has increasingly engaged itself in the economic policies of underdeveloped countries. It was not initially mandated to get involved in setting policy agendas in underdeveloped countries. Yash Tandon identifies that a withdrawal from this role would entail the IMF suspending its involvement in all of the following: Structural Adjustment Facility; Enhanced Structural Adjustment Facility; Structural Adjustment Programmes; Poverty Reduction Strategy Papers; the imposition of so-called good governance policies; loans for purposes other than the IMF's original mandate of addressing short-term external trade imbalances; bail-outs of banks and private lenders; and advice, prescriptions and mandates on national economic policies.[29]

However, for as long as the global economic system produces shocks that undermine poor countries' economies, the IMF may still have a role. One suggestion is that its operations should be devolved from Washington to regional blocs, such as the African Union.[30] These blocs could co-ordinate mutual financing to mitigate external shocks among the regional states. The IMF's role would then be limited to co-ordinating the functions of these regional blocs, in the management of global reserve funds. The power to intervene in crises would however rest with the regional members of each bloc. An arrangement along these lines would mitigate the perception, widespread in the Global South, that the IMF is an instrument of imperial domination. This would also democratise its functions. Alternative structures to the IMF are already starting to emerge, such as the Venezuelan Banco Del

Sur. It has been joined by a number of interested Latin American parties and aims to provide an alternative source of finance to the IMF in times of crisis. It is funded from Venezuelan oil revenues.[31]

South-South development co-operation has grown in importance in recent years. It demonstrates a real hope of breaking the DAC hold on development finance. A good example of South-South co-operation is the construction of the trans-Latin America oil pipeline, currently in progress.[32] The aim of this project is to redirect the resources within the region to development objectives. The focus is on objectives prioritised within the region, rather than allowing the wealth of the region to be expropriated by foreign MNCs. Certain countries in Latin America provided credit to others during the 2008 oil price crisis, again signalling the emergence of a new era of South-South co-operation. This co-operation challenges the traditional donors' role and authority as the sole providers of development finance. It serves to break the monopoly and, in doing so, transfers powers southwards.

China has become a major player in development finance, offering ODA to African countries in particular, with no policy conditions attached. There exists a range of perspectives on China's reasons for getting involved in providing development finance to Africa, summarised here:

Development partnership: driven by China's own economic needs (especially in terms of future food security) and a desire to transmit development expertise, with the aim of developing effective co-operative partnerships between Southern nations, toward mutual development.

Resource grabbing: from which point of view Chinese involvement in Africa is seen as a short term resource grab, with little concern for local needs and interests, human rights or development.[33]

Colonisation: An attempt to displace the Western orientation of African states and to forge political as well as economic control over them, through developing relationships with African elites.[34]

31. Ibid., Sader, 2008
32. Sader, 2008
33. see Grain, 2008
34. Alden, 2007:5-6

While these competing explanations differ wildly, there is no doubt that China's increasing involvement in Africa is offering a competing source of development finance. Ultimately, the choice that this offers countries in the South could provide them with greater leverage over the DAC donors. One can hope that this will help rebalance some of the inequitable relationships between the DAC donors and recipient countries. There also remains the possibility that China could offer appropriate expertise and technology to recipient countries, given its recent experience of rapid development. However, China's involvement in perpetuating the conflict in Sudan must surely give cause for concern about its intentions as a donor. There is a real risk that if China positioned itself as the main source of development finance, she might start to slip into the same, unfair arrangements and conditions that have proved so controversial and detrimental.

Similarly, China, Brazil, South Africa and India, along with a number of other countries, have begun to make financial and technological transfers to each other. These have taken the form of 'solidarity' transfers rather than simply commercial transactions.[35] Tandon uses the term 'solidarity' when describing these transfers to highlight what he perceives as their ideological aim: which is mutual co-operation to resist imperial domination by countries of the Global North. Included within this definition is aid that was given by China, India, Cuba and the USSR in support of anti-colonial struggles in Africa.[36] Ultimately, South-South cooperation of the sort described here could weaken and break the dominant role of the DAC in setting the agenda in the Global South. This would allow the people of Southern countries more autonomy in setting the agenda for their own development. In a world in which donors promoted the cause of social justice, the DAC would be forced to recognise the appropriateness of South-South and 'solidarity' co-operation and seek to promote it as an alternative to continued flows of ODA from its own members. Interconnectedness is at the heart of the concert of globalisation. In the long term the Global North countries will rely increasingly

35. Tandon 2008:125
36. Ibid, 39

on countries in the Global South. It is very short-sighted of developed nations to endanger the relationships they have with underdeveloped countries by exploiting them as unfairly as they do today. These countries are discovering that there are options available to them. They recognise that traditional sources of aid and 'support' are not necessarily their best options.

Global financial markets have entered into a crisis. This has called into question much of the basis for the general agreement that has dominated development thinking in recent years. The thinking insists that liberalised global trade and financial markets will bring about sustained economic growth that will end world poverty. This book has evidenced that even in times of global economic growth, this consensus rests more on ideology than reason. Global economic growth has failed to bring about poverty reduction in the Global South. This is primarily because this growth was achieved on the back of large scale extraction of wealth from the poor in the Global South. This ideology has allowed less scrupulous, less benevolent powerful elites to increase their wealth and power bases. ODA has been a key instrument in facilitating this. It has enabled elites to gain control of economic policy making in the Global South, for their own benefit. Economic growth has now stalled, amidst the greatest global economic crisis since the Great Depression. The ideology has been undermined, even according to its own terms, within its own make believe logic.

This presents an unprecedented global challenge and perhaps an unprecedented global opportunity for the forging of new social movements. It represents an opportunity to forge new relations between people based on solidarity, equality and social justice. Even if global financial markets survive their current crisis, and there are strong indications that they will, the future holds no reason to be optimistic for the kind of growth rates advocates of the MDG project suggest are necessary.

Economic growth requires the through-put of finite, limited resources, entailing the generation of pollution. The consequences of pollution are, primarily, displaced onto the Global South. Economic growth is by definition ultimately unsustainable. The environmental limits to global economic growth certainly will pose serious challenges. There is much debate about where these limits rest. However, all sides of the debate seem to acknowledge key challenges: peak oil, climate change, peak water and pressure on ecosystems around the world. An environmental limit to global economic growth must be reached at some point. The only question is when.[37] Ultimately, a new approach must come about and new social formations will be required. As Harvey commented:

> There are good reasons to believe that there is no alternative to a new global order of governance that will eventually have to manage the transition to a zero growth economy.[38]

Whatever one might think of Harvey's follow through statement, 'if that is to be done in an equitable way, then there is no alternative to socialism or communism',[39] there is certainly merit in recognising the limits of the current economic model.

Perhaps readers might be tempted to throw up their hands, despairing that the alternatives to ODA put forward in this chapter are too idealistic while the elites are too powerful. The reality is, however, that there *are* alternatives to the current model of ODA. Some of these alternatives are currently meeting resistance from powerful interest groups. Others, especially those organised within and between developing nations, are gaining in popularity and practice. Perhaps, however, the greatest opportunity lies within the growth constraints of the current global economic model. What might be considered idealistic today will gain in relevance as a new, more equitable, global reality is forced by the limits of the very economic model that supported inequality.

Meanwhile, the voting public, that powerful group of individuals who hold influence in their home countries, retain the right and privilege to hold their governments accountable for the effectiveness of their expenditure on ODA. In every democracy, the electorate has the privilege of shaping policy by making their

---

37. see, for example, Daly 1996
38. Harvey 2009
39. Ibid

opinions known. That privilege brings with it the opportunity to ask questions concerning the volume and nature of ODA budgets and demanding that they are used effectively for the elimination of inequality.

References/Bibliography

Acharya, Arnad; De Lima, Ana Teresa Fuzzo; Moore, Mick (2006) 'Proliferation and Fragmentation: transaction costs and the value of aid', *Journal of Development Studies*, Vol. 42, No.1, January, pp.1-21.

Alden, Chris, (2007) *China in Africa*, p 5-6, London: Zed.

Asian Development Bank report (2007) 'Purchasing Power Parity: Preliminary Report', online at www.adb.org, accessed November, 2009.

Bello, Walden (2009) *The Food Wars*, London: Verso.

Biccum, April R. (2005) 'Development and the 'New' Imperialism: a reinvention of colonial discourse in DFID promotional literature', *Third World Quarterly*, Vol 26, No 6, pp 1005-1020.

Boas, Morten and McNeill, Desmond (2003) *Multilateral Institutions – a critical introduction*, London: Pluto.

Brodie, Janine (1994) 'Shifting the Boundaries: gender and the politics of restructuring', in, Isabella Barker (ed) *The Strategic Silence: gender and economic policy*, London: Zed.

Buckland, Jerry (2004) *Ploughing up the Farm – neoliberalism, modern technology and the state of the world's farmers*, London: Zed.

Bulir, A. and Hamann, A. J. (2001) *How Volatile and Unpredictable are Aid Flows, and What are the Policy Implications?* IMF Working Papers 01/167, Washington DC: IMF.

Bulir, A. and Hamann, A. J. (2005) *Volatility of Development Aid: from the frying pan into the fire?*, Paper prepared for the seminar on Foreign Aid and Macroeconomic Management, organised by the IMF Institute and African Department, March 14-15, Maputo.

Bulir, A. and Lane, T. (2002) *Aid and Fiscal Management*, IMF WP/02/112. Washington DC: IMF.

Burnside, Craig and Dollar, David (1997) 'Aid, Policies and Growth', *World Bank Policy Research Working Papers*, 1777, Washington DC: World Bank.

Bush, Ray (2007) *Poverty & Neoliberalism – persistence and reproduction in the Global South*, London: Pluto.

Carbone, Maurizio (2007) *The European Union and International Development: the politics of foreign aid*, Oxon: Routledge.

Chang, Ha-Joon (2007) *Bad Samaritans – the guilty secrets of rich nations & the threat to global prosperity*, London: Random House.

Chhotray, Vasudha and Hulme, David (2009) 'Contrasting Visions for Aid and Governance in the 21st Century: the White House Millennium Challenge Account and DFID's Drivers of Change', *World Development*, Vol 37, No 1, pp 36-49.

Christian Aid, (2008) 'The Morning After the Night Before: the impact of the financial crisis on the developing world', *Christian Aid Report*, November, online at: www.christianaid.org.uk.

Collier, Paul (2006) 'Is Aid Oil? an analysis of whether Africa can absorb more aid', *World Development*, Vol 34, No 9, pp 1482-1497.

DAC, (2009) *Managing Aid: practices of DAC member countries*, Paris: OECD Publishing.

Das, Raju J. (2002) 'The Green Revolution and Poverty: a theoretical and empirical examination of the relationship between technology and society', *Geoforum*, Vol 33, pp 55-72.

Davis, Mike (2006) *Planet of Slums*, London: Verso.

Degnbol-Martinussen, John and Engberg-Pedersen, Poul (2003) *Aid – understanding international development cooperation*, London: Zed.

Dehesa, Guillermo de le (2006) *Winners and Losers in Globalization*, Oxford: Blackwell.

Dierckxsens, Wim (2000) *The Limits of Capitalism – an approach to globalization without neoliberalism*, London: Zed.

Djankov, Simeon; Montalvo, Jose G. and Reynal-Querol, Marta (2008) 'The Curse of Aid', *Journal of Economic Growth*, Vol 13, pp 169-194.

Duménil, Gérard and Lévy, Dominique (2004) 'The Economics of US Imperialism at the Turn of the 21st Century', *Review of International Political Economy*, Vol 11, No 4, October, pp 657-676.

Editorial (2005) 'Study Challenges Abstinence as an HIV Prevention Strategy', *Reproductive Health Matters*, Vol 13, No 26, November, pp 178-179.

Ellis, Frank (1992) *Agricultural Policies in Developing Countries*, Cambridge: Cambridge University Press.

Essex, Jamey (2008) 'Deservedness, Development and the State: Geographic categorization in the US Agency for International Development's foreign assistance framework', *Geoforum*, Vol 39, pp 1625-1636.

Foster, M and Keith, A (2004) *Linking Budget Support to Progress Towards Education MDGs and EFA Goals*, London: DFID.

Freebairn, Donald K. (1995) 'Did the Green Revolution Concentrate Incomes? a quantitative study of research reports', *World Development*, Vol 23, No 2, pp 265-279.

Gersham, John and Irwan, Alec (2000) 'Getting a Grip on the Global Economy', in , J. Y. Kim, J. V. Mullen, A. Irwin, J. Gershman (eds) *Dying for Growth: global inequality and the health of the poor*, Monroe, Maine: Common Courage Press, pp 11-43.

Glennie, Jonathan (2008) *The Trouble with Aid – why less could mean more for Africa*, London: Zed.

Gold, Lorna (2005) 'Are the Millennium Development Goals Addressing the Underlying Causes of Injustice: understanding the risks of the MDGs', *Trócaire Development Review*, Dublin, online at: www.trocaire.org, pp.23-41, accessed November, 2009.

Grain (2008) 'Making a Killing from Hunger: we need to overturn food policy now', *Grain Briefing*, April, 2008, online at http://www.grain.org/articles_files/atg-16-en.pdf, accessed August, 2009.

Harvey (2009) 'Organizing for the Anti-Capitalist Transition', available online at: www.davidharvey.org, accessed January, 2009.

Harvey, David (2005) *A Brief History of Neoliberalism*, Oxford: Oxford University Press.

Hayter, Theresa (1990) *The Creation of World Poverty*, London: Pluto.

Hayter, Theresa and Watson, Catherine (1985) *Aid – rhetoric and reality*, London: Pluto.

Hemson, David; Kassim Kulindwa, Haakon Lein & Adolfo Mascarenhas (eds) (2008) *Poverty and Water – explorations of the reciprocal relationship*, London: Zed.

Hyden, Goran (2008) 'After the Paris Declaration: taking on the issue of power', *Development Policy Review*, Vol 26, No 3, pp 259-174.

International Fund for Agricultural Development (IFAD) (2001), *Rural Poverty Report 2001: the challenge of ending rural poverty*, Rome, online at www.ifad.org/poverty/, accessed November, 2009.

Kaplinsky (2005) *Globalization, Poverty and Inequality: between a rock and a hard place*, Cambridge: Polity.

Kilby, Christopher (2009) 'The political economy of conditionality: an empirical analysis of World Bank loan disbursements', *Journal of Development Economics*, (89), pp 51-61.

Kono, Daniel Yuichi and Montinola, Gabriella R. (2009) 'Does Foreign Aid Support Autocrats, Democrats, or Both?', *The Journal of Politics*, Vol 71, No 2: pp 704-718.

Lines, Thomas (2008) *Making Poverty: a history*, London: Zed.

Madeley, John (1999) *Big Business Poor People – the impact of transnational corporations on the world's poor*, London: Zed.

Mavrotas, George and McGillivray, Mark (2009) 'Development Aid: Expectations, Effectiveness and Allocation', in, George Mavrotas and Mark McGillivray (eds) *Development Aid: A Fresh Look*, Basingstoke: Palgrave MacMillan.

McMichael (2008) *Development and Social Change – a global perspective* (4th ed.), Los Angeles: Pine Forge Press (Sage).

Moss, Todd J. (2007) *African Development: making sense of the issues and actors*, Boulder: Lynne Rienner.

Moyo, Dambisa (2009) *Dead Aid: why aid is not working and how there is another way for Africa*, London: Penguin.

Ndaruhutse, Susy and Brannelly Laura (2006) 'The Role of Donors in Creating Aid Volatility and How to Reduce it', Save the Children UK, available online at: eurodad.org, accessed: September, 2009.

Obadan, Mike I. (2008) *The Economic and Social Impact of Privatisation of State-owned Enterprises in Africa*, Dakar: CODESRIA.

OECD (2009), *Development Cooperation Report, 2009*, available online at: http://oberon.sourceoecd.org/vl=9522315/cl=29/nw=1/rpsv/dac09/index.htm, accessed: December, 2009.

OECD, (2009) 'International Development Statistics (IDS) online databases on aid and other resource flows', online at www.oecd.org/dac/stats/idsonline, accessed, December 2009.

OECD, (2009), Website of the Development Assistance Committee of the Organisation for Economic Co-operation and Development: online at www.oecd.org/dac, accessed 14/11/2009.

Pettifor, Ann (2001) 'Debt', in Emma Bircham and John Charlton (eds), *Anti-Capitalism – a guide to the movement*, London: Bookmarks.

Picciotto (2009) 'Development Effectiveness: An Evaluation Perspective', in George Mavrotas and Mark McGillivray (eds) *Development Aid: A Fresh Look*, Basingstoke: Palgrave MacMillan.

Pogge, T. W. and Reddy, S. G. (2002), 'How Not to Count the Poor', online at www.socialanalysis.org, accessed November, 2009.

Porteous, Tom (2005) 'British Government Policy in sub-Saharan Africa under New Labour', *International Affairs*, Vol 81, No 2, pp 281-297.

Pronk, J. (2003) 'Collateral Damage or Calculated Default? The Millennium Development Goals and the Policies of Globalisation', Inaugural Address, Institute of Social Studies: The Hague.

Razavi, Shahara (1999) 'Seeing Poverty Through a Gender Lens', *International Social Science Journal*, No 162, 1999, pp 473-482.

Rostow, W. W. (1960) *The Stages of Economic Growth – a non-communist manifesto*, London: Cambridge University Press.

Sachs, Jeffrey (2005) *The End of Poverty: how we can make it happen in our lifetime*, London: Penguin Books.

Sader, Emir (2008) 'The Weakest Link: neoliberalism in Latin America', *New Left Review*, Vol 52, July / August, 2008.

Schmidt, R. (2001) 'Efficient Capital Controls', *Journal of Economic Studies*, Vol 28, No 3, pp 199-212.

Schoepf, Brooke G.; Schoepf, Claude; Millen, Joyce V. (2000) 'Theoretical Therapies, Remote Remedies – SAPs and the political ecology of Poverty and Health in Africa', in, Jim Yong Kim (ed) *Dying for Growth – global inequality and the health of the poor*, Monroe Maine: Common Courage Press.

Sen, Amartya (1981) *Poverty and Famines: an essay on entitlement and famines*, Oxford: Clarendon.

Soederberg, Susan (2004) 'American Empire and 'Excluded States': the Millennium Challenge Account and the shift to pre-emptive development', *Third World Quarterly*, Vol 25, No 2, pp 279-302.

Sogge, David (2002) *Give and Take: what's the matter with foreign aid?*, London: Zed.

Spahn, P. B. (1996) 'The Tobin Tax and Exchange Rate Stability', *Finance & Development*, June, Washington: IMF.

Spicker, Paul, Sonia Alvarez Leguizamón & David Gordon (eds) (2006) *Poverty: an international glossary* (2nd ed), London: Zed.

Spratt, Stephen (2006) 'A Sterling Solution: implementing a stamp duty on sterling to finance international development', for the Stamp out Poverty Campaign, available online at: www.waronwant.org, accessed: January, 2009.

Storey, Andy and Williams, Simon (2006) *An Irish Development Bank?* A paper prepared for Dóchas, available online at: www.dochas.ie/Pages/Resources/documents/Irish_Development_bank.pdf, accessed 08 January, 2010.

Tandon, Yash (2008) *Ending Aid Dependence*, Oxford: Fahuma – Networks for Social Justice.

The Leprosy Mission (2009) *The Millennium Development Goals: unrealistic and unattainable because MDG implementation policies advance the interests of the rich world at the expense of the poor?* Online at www.leprosymission.ie, accessed, 14/11/2009.

Todaro, Michael P. and Smith, Stephen C. (2003) *Economic Development* (8th ed), Essex: Pearson Education.

UK Government (2005) 'Partnerships for poverty reduction: rethinking conditionality: A UK policy paper' Available online at: http://www.dfid.gov.uk/Documents/publications/conditionality.pdf, accessed 07 January, 2010.

UN Millennium Project (2005) *Investing in Development: a practical plan to achieve the Millennium Development Goals, overview*, New York: United Nations.

UN Millennium Project (2005) *Investing in Development: a practical plan to achieve the Millennium Development Goals*, London: Earthscan.

UNCTAD (2009) 'Keeping ODA Afloat: no stone unturned', *UNCTAD Policy Briefs*, No 7, March.

UNDP (1995) *Human Development Report 1995*, New York: United Nations.

UNDP (2007) *Human Development Report 2007-2008*, New York: United Nations.

UNDP (2008) *The Millennium Development Goals Report*, New York: United Nations.

UN-HABITAT (2006) *The State of the World's Cities Report 2006/2007: the Millennium Development Goals and urban sustainability - 30 years of shaping the habitat agenda*, London: Earthscan.

UNICEF (2009) *State of the World's Children Report*, online at http://www.unicef.org, accessed, November, 2009.

Vidal, John (2009), 'Analysis: Copenhagen draft text', *The Guardian* Newspaper, Friday 18 December, 2009.

Vreeland, James, Raymond (2003) *The IMF and Economic Development*, Cambridge: Cambridge.

Wade (2008) 'Is Globalization Reducing Poverty and Inequality', in Sharad Chari and Stuart Corbridge (eds), *The Development Reader*, Abingdon: Routledge.

Weis, Tony (2007) *The Global Food Economy – the battle for the future of farming*, London: Zed.

White, Howard (2009) 'Evaluating Aid Impact', in George Mavrotas and Mark McGillivray (eds) *Development Aid: A Fresh Look*, Basingstoke: Palgrave MacMillan.

Woodward, David and Andrew Simms (2006) 'Growth is Failing the Poor: the unbalanced distribution of the benefits and costs of global economic growth', *DESA Working Papers*, March, No 20, United Nations, online at: http://un.org/esa/desa/papers.

World Bank (2004) *The Millennium Development Goals for Health: rising to the challenges*, Washington DC: World Bank.

Zacune, Joe (2006) *Globeleq: the alternative report*, War on Want, available online at: www.waronwant.org.

Acronyms used in this book

AAA	Accra Action Agenda
ACP	African Caribbean Pacific
ADB	Asian Development Bank
AfDB	African Development Bank
ANC	African National Congress
CFA	Commission for Africa
DAC	Development Assistance Committee
DFID	Department for International Development
EDFI	European Development Finance Institutions
EU	European Union
FCO	Foreign and Commonwealth Office
G20	Group of 20 most Industrialised Countries
G8	Group of eight most Industrialised Countries
GDP	Gross Domestic Product
GNI	Gross National Income
GNP	Gross National Product
HDI	Human Development Index
HIPC	Heavily Indebted Poor Country Initiative
HYV	High Yielding Variety
IBRD	International Bank for Reconstruction and Development (World Bank)
IDB	Inter-American Development Bank
IFAD	International Fund for Agricultural Development
IFIs	International Financial Institutions
IMF	International Monetary Fund
IPRs	Intellectual Property Rights
LCDs	Least Developed Countries
LICs	Low Income Countries
MCA	Millennium Challenge Account
MDGs	Millennium Development Goals
MNC	Multi National Corporation
NGO	Non Governmental Organisation
ODA	Overseas Development Aid
OECD	Organisation for Economic Co-operation and Development
OEIs	Official Equity Investments
OPEC	Organisation of Petroleum Export Countries
PDAE	Paris Declaration of Aid Effectiveness
PPP	Purchasing Power Parity
PRSPs	Poverty Reduction Strategy Programmes

SAPs	Structural Adjustment Programmes
SMEs	Small and Medium Enterprises
TRIMs	Trade Related Investment Measures
TRIPs	Trade Related Aspects of Intellectual Property Rights
UK	United Kingdom
UN	United Nations
UNDP	United Nations Development Programme
UNHCR	United Nations High Commissioner for Refugees
UNICEF	United Nations Childrens' Fund
US	United States of America
USAID	United States Agency for International Development
WFP	World Food Programme
WTO	World Trade Organisation
WWII	World War II